Start, Write, and Finish Your First Novel

Alan Black

Books
By
Alan Black

Non-Fiction
How to Start, Write, and Finish Your First Novel

Western Novelette
A Cold Winter

Science Fiction
Chewing Rocks
Empty Space
Metal Boxes
Steel Walls and Dirt Drops
Titanium Texicans

General Fiction
Chasing Harpo

with Bernice Knight   *An Ozark Mountain Series*
The Friendship Stones (book one)
The Granite Heart (book two)
The Heaviest Rock (book three)

How to Start, Write, and Finish Your First Novel
Published by arrangement with the author

Printing History
© 2015 Copyright by Alan Black

Cover Design: The Cover Collection

ISBN-13: 978-1511522939
ISBN-10: 1511522933
Library of Congress: 1-2280913731

Dedication:

To everyone who has wanted to or has actually started writing their first novel, but never completed it. Maybe life interfered, or a case of writer's block occurred that you were never able to break through, or your story lost its way and you could never figure out how to get it back again. It's time to begin for the first time or blow the dust off that original manuscript you tossed into the desk drawer prior to your last move. Whatever you do, it's time to write something.

Acknowledgments:

A lot of wisdom went into this guide, most of it wasn't mine. I want to thank all of those writers who shared, discussed their craft, and taught me.

I would also like to thank A.J. Questerly (author of *Pangaea*) for her great oversight and beta read. A lot of thanks go to Jean Neal and Duann Black for their editorial expertise.

How to
Start, Write, and Finish Your First Novel

Alan Black

CreateSpace

Table of Contents

- Plot
- Brainstorming ideas
- Borrow storylines
- Plagiarism is a no-no

2.3 Write what we know and write what we read
- Personal focus
- Know our audience
- Select a specific genre
- Add what does not belong
- Make it personal

2.4 Build a frame
- Characters
- One sentence summary character exercise
- Descriptions
- Primary characters
- Secondary characters
- Tertiary characters
- Absent characters
- Character names
- Location
- Conversation

2.5 Never end a writing session unless our protagonist is in trouble
- Conflict
- Potential Conflict varieties
- Conflict flow
- Conflict resolution

2.6 Make bad things happen to our characters
- Trouble abounds
- Hooks
- Trouble is what fiction is all about
- Chapter hooks

- Write the climax first
- Back cover blurbs
- Write the back cover blurb exercise

SECTION THREE: KEEP AT IT

3.1 Only we can determine what helps or hinders our writing efforts
- Environment
- Distractions
- Tools
- Physical exercise
- Hydration
- Setting goals and rewards
- Schedule active writing time
- Length of time
- Scheduling time blocs
- Make writing a habit

3.2 Keep writing
- Writer's block
- Keep writing
- Do not edit
- Record our thoughts
- Record our observations
- Stay away from the internet
- Writer's block exercises

3.3 Find or start a writers group consistent with our genre and style
- Open writers' groups
- Closed or private writers' groups

3.4 Our first goal is to get our story written
- Points of view
- Outlining the story
- Timelines

- Avoid flashbacks
- Avoid data dumps
- Leave the punch line for the end

3.5 A perfect title

3.6 Author's name

SECTION FOUR: TYING IT ALL TOGETHER

4.1 Are we finished?
- Prologues
- Chapters
- Quotes
- Word count
- Journaling

4.2 Where to stop
- Don't cheat our reader out of a good ending
- Story theft
- Copyright

SECTION FIVE: WRAPPING IT UP

5.1 Final Points
- Grammar and editing
- Editors
- Verbal feedback
- Story gaps
- Technical gaffs
- Vocabulary
- Show, don't tell
- Sentences
- Rhythm

5.2 Write fast; rewrite slow
- Editing
- Proofreading
- Punctuation
- Grammar
- Formatting
- Agents
- Publishers and publishing
- Parting words

Appendix: Figures of Speech

About the author

Praise for books by Alan Black

If you have any young friends who aspire to become writers, the second greatest favor you can do them is to present them with copies of 'The Elements of Style'. The first greatest, of course, is to shoot them now, while they're happy. (Dorothy Parker, American writer and poet)

SECTION ONE: INTRODUCTION

1.1 FICTION WRITING HAS NO RULES

PURPOSE OF THIS BOOK

Many authors look at other authors as competition. I don't. We're in this together. We're going to work together until we have your first book completed, pulled from where stories hide and in a readable form.

This book is a conglomeration of my notes placed here to help new writers finish their first novel. It is designed to help aspiring writers do exactly what the title states—to start, to write, and to finish. It will help us become writers who have completed their first novel. I say us because I'll be here with you throughout the journey. We'll travel this path together to the successful completion of your first novel. This small book won't teach us everything we need to know to become a successful author. As with any long-term goal, the learning is in the doing. This book is designed to help us get to doing.

We're writing to write, even if it never sells. Our goal isn't about writing a novel that will be published. Publishing is a whole 'nother animal, and to push the metaphor a little, publishing is more like a porcupine than a fluffy kitten. Publishing isn't a requirement to becoming a writer, or an author, or a novelist. It's simply one of the ways to share our stories with others. We aren't writing to publish or writing just what will sell. To many, this may sound negative, but not to us. Our first book is a wonderful accomplishment all on its own, deserving of praise, awe, and wonder.

Learn as much by writing as by reading. (Sir John Dalberg-Acton)

Knowing grammar rules may make our storytelling easier to write, easier to read and easier to understand. However, there are already more than enough textbooks written about editing, proofreading, grammar, and formatting. I don't want to add to their number any more than we want to read another textbook. Included at the book's end are some brief comments about those subjects. As we learn the rules to editing, proofreading, grammar, and formatting, we also learn how and when we can break those rules. I have included a few tidbits about all of these things in this book, but primarily we have a higher purpose.

We are here because of our need to write, because we have stories we need to tell. Our need to write is the primary motivation for these tidbits, just as my need to write, drove me to write my first book years ago. It's your need to write that prompted you to pick up this book.

Go read a book if you don't need to write.

Our writing motivation is the story we feel compelled to tell that comes from our imagination, thoughts, and daydreams, from our heart, or from those scars we keep tucked away, either the ones hidden under our clothes or the ones buried deep under our skin, in our soul, and our id. That tale is the one eating away at us, internally screaming at us, jabbing at the base of our brain, poking at the muscles of our tongue, all in an effort to be told, to be put on paper, to be tossed into cyberspace.

"Everybody has a secret world inside of them. I mean everybody. All of the people in the whole world, I mean everybody — no matter how dull and boring they are on the outside. Inside them they've all got unimaginable, magnificent, wonderful, stupid, amazing worlds... Not just one world. Hundreds of them. Thousands, maybe." (Neil Gaiman)

We have to write our story to tell it; otherwise, it just comes out a jumbled mess. Our objective is to write our first fictional manuscript.

This book isn't a comprehensive list of everything a writer should know. That takes a lifetime of writing and hard work. What we have here are simply a few tidbits to help prime the pump, grease the wheels, clear the decks, and set the stage for anyone to get started as a writer.

Our design is to flip the switch in our brains from off the position where we simply think about writing a novel to the on position where we actually decide and take action towards that goal. I'm not saying thinking is bad; it's neither bad nor good. Thinking is the beginning of any activity, but no one has written the commercial software to turn our thoughts into words on paper ... yet.

To some of us, the wresting of beauty out of language is the only thing in the world that matters. (Anthony Burgess)

When we write, we have a story to tell. We tell that story by adding one word after another. The more words we add, the more precise our storytelling.

Writing matters. We may pay our bills by going to a day job, but we are writers. Live the part.

- Take it seriously.
- Pretend we are getting paid to finish.
- We are writers and we say we're writers if someone asks what we do.

VISION STATEMENT

Write a Vision Statement about being a writer. This is our vision, our dream and our fantasy. We need not share it with anyone else. This statement will verbalize two points.

- Why are we doing what we're doing?
  - o Are we writing for our joy?
  - o Are we writing to entertain others?
- What is our primary goal?
  - o Are we writing to become wealthy?
  - o Are we seeking fame?

Note: the two points in the vision statement may not be mutually exclusive.

This is my vision statement: "I want my readers amazed they missed sleep because they could not put down my book. I want my readers amazed that I made them laugh on one page and cry on the next. I want to give my readers a pleasurable respite from the cares of the world for a few hours. I want to write the book that I would want to read."

FICTION IS

Fiction may combine known facts, truths, and accuracies. We, as writers, twist and alter existing elements and turn them into fiction.

Fiction is imaginative literature in narrative form. It's imagined or re-imagined, invented or re-invented or simply made-up. Yes, our story may take place on a dusty west Texas road with a tired old cowboy in a tired old pickup truck. We may have driven that road, we may have seen that cowboy, and we may even drive that old truck to work every day. However, our plan as a wordsmith is to take that reality and twist it to the purpose of our story.

It is often said that one has but one life to live, but that is nonsense. For one who reads, there is no limit to the number of lives that may be lived, for fiction, biography and history offer an inexhaustible number of lives in many parts of the world, in all periods of time. (Louis L'Amour)

We postulate fiction for the purpose of entertainment, argument, and explanation. Trust me when I say that most fiction wordsmiths do not write for the money. There may be some cash here and there, but a very small percentage of writers actually make much of it. I hope you are in that small percentage, if that is your goal.

FICTION IS NOT

Fiction is not magazine articles. Magazine articles are a form, not the product itself. It isn't poetry. It isn't a biography, autobiography, or historiography. However, a good writer may couch his or her fiction in any one of these forms or points of view.

Fiction isn't stream of consciousness writing. That's just literary diarrhea. It may be, and I stress may be, a valid form of literary exercise, but watching someone do pushups can be as boring as watching the same television commercial for the umpteenth time in the last hour. This also can be a valid point of view to a storyline when a character has no mental filters, but no one wants to read a writer's personal stream of consciousness, except the writer's mother or psychoanalyst.

Fiction isn't creation. Creation is making something out of nothing. Creation is the bailiwick of God and astrophysicists. We do not write from nothing, the words are all out there. We just have to put them in the order that best pleases us and may please our readers.

FICTION WRITING HAS NO RULES
Fiction writing has no rules. Our creative writing teacher in the seventh grade may have tried to beat us over the head with a rulebook, but rules are nonsense. There isn't any rule that can't be broken; there isn't any rule that hasn't been successfully broken; and there isn't any rule that the gods of literature shouldn't repeal. What matters is the story we are trying to tell and our story's connection with our audience.

Writing fiction can be emotionally cathartic, mentally taxing, a waste of time, a passionate hobby and/or all of these things, individually or in any combination.

Rule number one—There are no rules to writing fiction.

Remember: when people tell you something's wrong or doesn't work for them, they are almost always right. When they tell you exactly what they think is wrong and how to fix it, they are almost always wrong. (Neil Gaiman)

However, having said that, I must point out the following: copy editors have rules. Boy! Do they have rules. Their bibles are *The Chicago Manual of Style* and Strunk and White's *The Elements of Style*. Their combined length is over 1000 pages. They want us to know where that dreaded Oxford comma goes and the proper use of a dangling participle.

<u>Rule number two</u>—We can't fix what ain't been writ.

If we stop to learn these rules, it'll be decades, if ever, before we finish our novel. Ignore the rules for now. Fix these small mistakes later.

Beta readers also have rules. Mainly, a beta reader's job is to ensure our story flows smoothly from beginning to end. There's a great benefit to having more than one set of eyes on a story. These people are a necessary evil in writing.

Research is a time killer in the early stages of our first novel. Just Write.

<u>Rule number three</u>—We don't have to write our novel from the first word to the last period.

We can write our novel in any order, any direction, any storyline flow we want. We should write the gunfight first if that is what we see the clearest. Write the space battle if that is what we have diagrammed out and it excites us. Write the love scene first if that's what is burning in our … well, the point is, we write in any order we want and then go back to connect our scenes and fill in those gaps. But, we won't have gaps later if we don't write something now. Beta readers will help us spot those gaps we have gone mind-blind to.

Content/Technical editors have rules. Yes. We need to know the .22 caliber rifle we have our heroine shooting doesn't have a safety selector. But, don't take the time to research it now.

Literary agents have rules. Um ... nobody knows what these rules are, but they have them. It's kind of like a secret society where we aren't told the rules unless we join and we can't join until we know the rules. We write for ourselves, not for agents.

Publishers have rules. Yep. The same rules apply here as for literary agents. They are wonderful people, but we're not writing our novel for them.

Booksellers have rules. Mostly their rules involve our writing something that sells using a clear genre that makes our novel easy to place on their shelves. Seriously, they won't know what to do with a mystery about a romantic couple fighting hordes of zombies with the Roman legions.

Even our dear readers, our customers, our intended audience have rules. There is a rhythm and flow to most genres. We already hear this rhythm if we read the genre we write.

Ignore these rules. Write.

We learn everybody's rules by progressing in skill and maturing as authors. We're writers, not marketing agents; that comes later. For the sake of our first manuscript's rough draft, let's write as if we have forgotten all of the rules. In the long run, as we rewrite, edit and prepare for possible readers, we will review those rules, but for now:

- Forget about punctuation or ending a sentence with a preposition, just write the sentence.
- Forget about whether a tertiary character in chapter four was named Tammie and spelled Tammy in chapter fourteen, just write the chapter.
- Forget about keeping our manuscript between 60,000 and 120,000 words, just write the manuscript.

Rule number four—The story takes as long to tell as it takes.

Just remember, it is our story and no one should tell us when it starts, when it finishes, and how long it should take to get to the end. Word counts have their uses, but not at the expense of delaying our writing.

- Forget about whether the market is flooded with books about teenage wizards. Just write.
- We should even forget about mixing romantic elements into a western novel. Don't be so genre specific that we miss the diversity in our character's lives. Just write.

Get through a draft as quickly as possible. Hard to know the shape of the thing until you have a draft. Literally, when I wrote the last page of my first draft of "Lincoln's Melancholy" I thought, Oh, shit, now I get the shape of this. But I had wasted years, literally years, writing and re-writing the first third to first half. The old writer's rule applies: Have the courage to write badly. (Joshua Wolf Shenk)

Our primary concern in writing that elusive first rough draft is to get it written. Our first draft will most likely be rough as an old cob. For those of us who don't understand the origins of "rough as an old cob", it's from the old days when wooden outhouses—toilets—were located behind the house. We might have to resort to using an old, dry corncob if we've already used the last page of last year's Sears, Roebuck and Company catalog as toilet paper. That is rough indeed.

The first draft of everything is shit. (Ernest Hemingway)

Recently, I have heard many a writer recently refer to this stage of a manuscript as zero draft. It's true that no one—and I mean no one—should see this draft. It's for us and no one else. It's the completion of our imaginative story telling. It's the end result of our goal to write our first novel. Believe me, we will want to clean it up before we even share any of it with our advisory group and alpha readers. For the purposes in this collection of writing tips, I'll continue to call it the first draft, if for nothing more than ordinal consistency.

Rough is okay in our first draft. Rough is what we seek. Rough is our goal. We can fix rough. We cannot fix what does not exist. Writing is a muddy swamp of creative juices mixed with heavy clods of imagination. Therefore, ignore the rules.

WORDSMITHY

The words we use as wordsmiths are all there for the taking. They're in our heads, our dictionaries and our thesauruses. How many words do we know? Words are the tools we use to make our finished product. Just as a carpenter cannot build a house with tools he does not have; a wordsmith cannot use tools that are not in the toolbox.

However, that doesn't mean we should use every tool we own. We're all wordsmiths. We all use the tools with varying degrees of skill. An auto mechanic has a toolbox full of tools. A good auto mechanic will use the proper tool for a repair job. A backyard grease monkey may use a socket wrench and eyeball tightening a bolt. A certified auto technician will use a torque wrench to tighten the bolt to specifications so as not to under- or over-tighten the bolt. Use the right word at the right time and you'll write a smoother tale.

How many tools do we have in our toolboxes? We can only use the words we know. We should only use the words our readers know. This is part and parcel of selecting our intended audience. We don't want our reader to stop reading and go to a dictionary.

Never use jargon words like reconceptualize, demassification, attitudinally, judgmentally. They are hallmarks of a pretentious ass. (David Ogilvy)

What is the reading level of our intended audience? I dare say, if we look to find a valid and consistent study on the subject of average reading levels, we'll be no less baffled at the end of our search. I've seen studies that say the average person reads at a sixth grade level, and that the average high school graduate reads at an eighth or ninth grade level.

We're concerned with the reading level of our intended target audience, not the average reader.

Are we writing for a grade from a college professor? Well, then—shoot for the moon. We use every tool in our box and we may even go out and rent a few more tools. But, if our desire is to write a novel for young adults or teens, we might want to curb the use of our fancy new electronic tools and go back to the basics.

As a wordsmith, we may have the word erudite in our toolbox. Should we use this word? Is our goal to make our reader stop and lookup new words and learn that erudite means having great knowledge or scholarly? How about if we just use the word smart, clever, intelligent, or bright?

The difference between the right word and the almost right word is the difference between lightning and a lightning bug. (Mark Twain)

Understand that a word must convey its meaning to the reader. Made up words are built within an existing language framework. For example, wordsmith is a known word. For a long time now, the blacksmith is the smithy, or at least since Henry Wadsworth Longfellow put the word in his poem *The Village Blacksmith*. Someone, somewhere, and some-when jammed two words together to make a new word having a different meaning. We can do the same thing as needed. We should not write "John was a crantwister" without explaining the term crantwister.

What is the point of writing if our reader does not continue reading? The characters who inhabit our stories are in the world. They aren't in attendance in the exact form we describe them, but they're someone we know, someone we've met or someone we've read about. As writers, our characters—whether human, animal, plant or mutant zombie alien from outer space—must have some characteristic that allows our readers to like-love-dislike-hate them. Our readers must feel some connection to continue reading.

The description of places comes from our memories and imaginations, but our job is to make these words flow into our reader's minds like clear spring water rushing down a small mountain stream. The places we write about are there—somewhere. They are places our reader has been to or would like to go to, or would avoid going to again at all costs. A big dead skunk rotting in the water spoils the view, just like adding a word that doesn't belong. Conversely, a missing rock can spoil the sound just like a missing word can spoil our picture because it's the rocks in the stream that cause a brook to sing.

Again, we may have been to Texas. We may have even met a real working cowboy. We may drive a truck to work every day. What we do as wordsmiths is to use these mental images and massage them into our storylines. Our reader may not have travelled west of the Atlantic Ocean, but our job is to help transfer our mental images to them. Our words describing a tired old cowboy driving a tired old blue pickup truck on a dusty west Texas dirt road will paint a picture directly into the minds of our readers.

1.2 TAKING A LONG TALK OFF A SHORT STORY

Many writers begin learning their craft by writing short stories. There's nothing wrong with short stories. Edgar Allen Poe believed all stories should be read in one sitting. Having said that, short stories are not what we are working towards. We didn't decide to write a novel in a vacuum. Most of us have tried our hand at this writing thing before this book caught our eye. We may have a drawer full of short stories lying around gathering dust, glaring at us with accusing stares, as if it's our fault no one ever gets to stroke their well-crafted words. You may be ahead of the curve if you can start your novel with these short stories.

We aren't here to discuss getting published, but for the sake of conversation with writers who are enamored of short stories, we should look at the short story volumes published today. All short story anthologies are from or about (in)famous people or (in)famous times. Many short story anthologies by unknown writers languish in the bottom of the writer's desk drawer for want of a reputable publisher.

However, a persistent and dedicated writer may get their short story anthology published by a print-on-demand (POD) publisher. They may—I stress may—sell enough books to earn enough royalties to pay for the upfront costs charged by their chosen POD publisher. Self-publishing is a valid option; however, short story anthologies continue to be difficult to successfully market.

There are many ways to beat this short story wilderness. I offer four suggestions for turning a stack of short stories into something other than dust collectors.

REWRITE

Take that favorite short story and re-write it into a full length novel. Do not add fluff or wordy descriptions. This is padding the story and believe me, readers recognize when a writer begins to slide away from the real story. Fluff can be as boring as reading technical specifications about fictional weapon systems.

Add conflict to the main character's life. Most of us have more than one bad thing happen at a time. How many facets do we have in our own lives? We're husbands and wives, we're employers and employees, we're sons and daughters, we're fathers and mothers, we're neighbors, customers, and strange faces on an elevator. Anything and everything can go wrong in any and every facet of our lives. It's the same for our characters. Conflict may also arise from secondary characters lives that have an impact on our protagonist.

RED THREAD

The red thread approach inserts one central character into each story. They need not be a prime character or even secondary character in every story. They just need to make an appearance. It might be as simple as our red thread character being a diner getting a second cup of coffee from the waitress who is that short story's main character, our red thread character is a young hooligan hiding behind a bush when he sees the short story's protagonist coming, or our red thread character is just a topic of idle conversation between characters in another short story.

A 20th century theologian coined the red thread when he hypothesized that Jesus Christ is the subject of every book of the Bible, even the Old Testament books, whether by direct prophesy, by subject matter or as a metaphor, thus the red thread ties each book to the next. Our red thread character may or may not interact with our short story characters, that's our choice.

SERIALIZATION

Let's assume our stories all gravitate toward the same genre and approximate locales. If not, we can change them. We can serialize the short story with a favorite character or an interesting location and place a little piece of that story into every subsequent short story, tying them all together.

James Michener used a specific location to tie stories together in *Centennial*. James R. Webb also used this method in his screenplay *How the West was Won* although the west was a pretty broad location and the story followed a specific family over many generations.

Serialization involves taking a favorite character from our best short story and putting them into every other short story in the anthology. Spreading the character across the whole collection generates a compelling story arc by their strength of character. We will look at two methods of serialization, both of which provide us a continuity of story arc.

First, we break our specially chosen short story into pieces. We then add a small piece into each remaining short story, completing the book and adding the conclusion to the serialized short story at the end of our last short story.

Second, we break our specially chosen short story into pieces and insert each segment between every other short story. Let's look at the formula for achieving this.

Step one: separate the short story to be serialized into segments. Step two: place the remaining fully completed short stories in the order that provides proper flow to the overall story arc. Step three: build the completed work by starting with the first serialized short story segments and adding to it the first short story. Next add the second serialized segment followed by the second short story. Repeat the process until the exciting conclusion in chapter fourteen of the final serialized short story segment.

Okay, since this may be difficult to follow, let's try an example.

This is a quick story outline about Bob, a cowboy who has taken on the task of breaking and training a rangy young horse for a nearby rancher. He has to perform the following tasks: restore the horse to good health, build-up the horse's trust in him, familiarize the horse to the bridle and tack, acclimate the horse to people, and present the fully trained horse to the rancher.

First, we break down Bob's story into six small sections and then intersperse previously written short stories between Bob's story sections. Here's the flow:

Bob has to bring the young horse back to good health.
The first short story is about Alice, a nurse working with a terminally ill child.

Bob has to earn the young horse's trust.
Next is a short story about Larry and the trust issues he has with his new part time employer at the garage.

Bob has to familiarize the young horse to the bridle and saddle.
The next short story is about a master painter teaching his apprentice to use the right medium for the correct effect.

Bob acclimates the horse to people.
Now insert the short story is about a former convict's reclamation to society.

Bob presents the fully trained young horse to the rancher.
Your last short story is about a young girl who didn't want to attend the beauty pageant her mother pushed her into entering.

Bob earns his reward.

We now have a novel length story combining thematic elements into a cohesive unit.

THE MINSTREL'S TALE METHOD

This method is named after Anna Questerly's wonderful young adult series, *The Minstrel's Tale*. The main character is telling us a story about a storyteller telling us stories. The main character gives us a hook to capture our reader's attention while telling us a story about the minstrel who sets the reader's hook deeper as he tells his own story interspersed with—you guessed it—stories he tells his audience within the story itself.

We adapt this method by giving our readers a character who ties our short stories together by telling his or her audience—and our readers by proxy—each story in turn. The stories may or may not be connected. That is the writer's decision. Do we style our work after *The Arabian Nights: Tales from a Thousand and One Nights* translated by Richard Burton or more like *The Martian Chronicles* by Ray Bradbury? It's our novel. It's our decision to make.

Don't loaf and invite inspiration; light out after it with a club, and if you don't get it you will nonetheless get something that looks remarkably like it. (Jack London)

SECTION TWO: GETTING STARTED

2.1 MAKING STUFF UP

STORY IDEAS

The most common question authors are asked is "where do your story ideas come from?" The answer isn't very enlightening to most non-writers. They have an overwhelmingly unenthusiastic response to my answer. Normally, writers shrug and say "I find story ideas from where all good storylines come from. There's a great big book in the library that gives you a list of possible story ideas. You just have to pick one that hasn't been used before." It's no secret that there isn't any such book.

You get ideas from daydreaming. You get ideas from being bored. You get ideas all the time. The only difference between writers and other people is we notice when we're doing it. (Neil Gaiman)

Story ideas come from anywhere and everywhere. Some examples are:
- Newspaper articles
- Bad television shows
- Dreams slightly remembered when waking
- Sudden insights while out for a long walk
- Good conversations
- Overheard conversations
- Conversations gone bad
- Strange locations

- The smell of fresh bread wafting through the air when there are no bakeries nearby
- Pictures of a body mangled by a car wreck with a bullet wound in his chest
- Putting a bullet through the head of a zombie at a hundred yards
- The feeling of touching an orange while wearing silk gloves
- Remembering the soft touch of Grandma's hand on your cheek
- Remembering the harsh touch of Grandpa's belt across your backside
- The back cover of a book that bore no relation to the story inside
- The sly glance of an attractive painted lady
- The rambunctious bounce of a puppy
- The taste of the color blue on a bright spring morning

All of these ideas and more can become wonderful stories with the added questions of how and why and what led to this. We can generate a storyline from work, an activity, a hobby, a newspaper article or a pastime. I wrote a science fiction novel called *Metal Boxes*. The idea for the story came about while I was working as the purchasing manager for a warehouse. I happened to read an article about how a purchasing manger had stolen 2.5 million dollars from his employer. The newspaper article was very specific about how he managed the theft. Wrangling boxes from one place to the next may not be exciting, but adding a theft with some real how-to information made for a better story. Note, I left that job just as broke as when I started working there.

A good storyline can come from a character or a location.

A character can be interesting because something happened to make the character who he / she is. The location may be interesting because of what happened there. "Ripped from Today's Headlines" is a common TV promotional blurb, because real stories can be more bizarre than fiction. They can also give a writer a rough storyline or a plot outline.

The difference between fiction and reality? Fiction has to make sense. (Tom Clancy)

Ideas are like rocks in the Ozarks—one can cross a forty-acre field by walking on the rocks and never touch dirt. Ideas surround us. We must work our imagination to see an idea fully and twist it into a story. When we have a nugget of a thought, a possible story idea, we should write it down. Quickly, try to do a complete brain dump on the page. Get it all written down before you forget it.

Don't talk about it. Write it down. There are two reasons for not talking about our story idea:

First: If we haven't completed our first novel, we may talk to people who may not be as enthusiastic as we are about our writing career. We do not need any negative influences at this point in our writing career.

Second: Talking about an idea can take the spark out of our imagination. We have talked it through and our mind will tell us that we're done with it. We take the idea, write it down and let it simmer, let it percolate, let it fester and only let it out through our fingertips.

Practice isn't the thing you do once you're good. It's the thing you do that makes you good. (Malcolm Gladwell and Frank Brady)

WHAT IF

Pure and simple conjecture is the *what if* method for kick starting story ideas. We generate hypothetical situations and allow our imaginations to run wild. Walking through a door is boring, but what comes next can be exciting and limited only by our imaginations. We only limit the situations by our ability as fiction writers.

What if you:
- tripped on a crack in the sidewalk
- ran a stop sign because you were not paying attention
- saw an accident on the side of the road
- stepped through a door
- decided to go to a ranch and ride a horse for the first time
- took the day off and played hooky at the zoo
- realized you didn't have a single book in the house to read that you hadn't already read
- opened the refrigerator only to find a half empty jar of dill pickles
- called your best friend
- were waiting in an endless line
- stepped through a door

Begin with our initial action and ask *what if*. What if we stepped through a door and:
- the room isn't there
- we find a room filled with clowns
- all our old girlfriends or boyfriends are in the room

- the door slams shut and locks behind us
- everyone in the room stands and applauds us for some unknown reason
- the room is filled with old folks and kittens and it's on fire
- gravity ceases to exist
- the room is filled with naked people waiting for us to arrive fully clothed
- the room is filled with eager students waiting to hang on our every word and we cannot speak
- our deceased grandfather is having a conversation with God while waiting for us to arrive
- a shot rings out and the bullet zips past our ear
- we trip over a body
- we see our spouse and our best friend locked in a passionate embrace

We design our model with a character and a place or thing. Above I have listed 13 possibilities. What are all the possible human reactions to any one of them?

Take a *what if* choice to your advisory group and ask for suggestions when you run into a particularly hoary story direction. Advisory group? At this stage, it's people who think outside the box, even to the extent of suggesting the ridiculous. This group of people will not throw negatives into the pot, but will be happy to explain why it would be possible to open a door and find nothing but a choice of other doors. Yes, I've said not to talk about our story nuggets, but this isn't a nugget. This is story generation from scratch.

If you don't like the road you're walking on, start paving another one. (Dolly Parton)

WHAT IF EXERCISE

List 10 actions taken after the phrase, "What if you".

List 10 new action statements beginning with "What if you stepped through a door and …"

DECISION TREE
A decision tree is a form of analysis used to choose between several courses of action when you are initially undecided. Decision trees help guide you in determining which choice is best for your current situation. We can adapt this in writing to develop a story tree. Begin by identifying alternative actions available to you. For example:

We walk down the street to the intersection and cannot decide which way to turn.
- turning left leads downtown to the business district
- turning right leads to the shopping mall with all its wonderful stores
- continuing straight ahead leads to the park where you can feed the ducks at the pond

To help us decide which choice to make, list the pros and cons of each alternative. Each alternative probably has more than one pro or con. Start diagramming this with the tree trunk (which way to turn), major tree limbs (left-business district, right-shopping mall, straight-park), branches from the limbs and leaves from the branches. Let's extend our example:

Decision Tree Trunk
    Which way to turn

Major tree limbs (major choices available)
    Left to business district
    Right to shopping mall
    Straight to park with pond

Branches shooting off from the limbs (pros and cons)
    Business district: boring, sidewalk cafes, no business to conduct
    Shopping mall: shoe stores, food court, movie theater, overcrowded, no parking
    Park: ducks to feed, shade trees along walking paths, relaxing solitude, too far to walk

Leaves (pros and cons of each branch) – I'll show just one example
    Ducks to feed: ducks are pushy, no money to buy duck feed, ducks are messy, ducks are too loud, ducks are cute, I can take pictures of the ducks to post online, I have cash in my pocket

It's now decision time. My choice is since today is Tuesday, and I have money burning a hole in my pocket, I'll go straight to the park to spend it on feeding the ducks.

We can make it as simple or detailed as we desire. We're looking at the decision in a systematic way and we've written some details to our choices. We now have a storyline, we've worked ourselves out of the literary corner we wrote for ourselves.

Don't discard the decision tree quite yet, hang on to it in case you need it later. We may realize our storyline needs refining and we may have to hack away at the tree and backup to the tree trunk and start from a different limb or the same limb but a different branch.

Decision tree analysis, sometimes called decision mapping, can provide effective *what if* results. We ask ourselves—if this happens, then what possible decision will our characters make? Ask the brains in our circle of influence to help us with a section of *what if* statements. I'm constantly amazed at the imagination of the average human when answering *what if*.

STORY FILE
As we search about for a storyline for our first novel, or your twenty-first, keep a story idea file. It doesn't matter what medium we use to store our storylines.

My first story file was written on 3 x 5 index cards. That quickly became a limiting medium, as there is only so much information that can be crammed onto an index card.

A three-ring binder would give us room, but it sounds like a lot of work, unless you really like the sound of a number two pencil on paper. The benefit to this is that no one has ever seen a three-ring binder crash and lose data. The binder itself can go missing, but that is a different issue all together.

I keep my storylines in a computer file. The computer gives me a lot of room to expand each storyline in my ideas file. It allows me to keep a file as short as a first paragraph or as long as the first four chapters. It allows me to put down as much information on story ideas as I have in my head. This is very helpful, because I find that I don't remember all of the details after a few years. One bit of advice—back up the file, chances are you will not remember every detail any better than I do if you have a computer crash.

Our story file should contain at least four sections:

1. Actual story or plot lines: we need to write as much of the story as we have available to refresh our memory when we review the file next month or next decade. It should also include any of those practice first paragraphs (we will discuss these later) that we deem worthy of salvaging from the dead file.

2. Unusual characters: descriptions, accents, mannerisms, and any peculiar personality flaws. Such people may not inhabit your current work, but they may be useful in another literary effort. These people may add a full-bodied heart to a later novel.

3. Unusual places: buildings, locales, parks, and peculiar backyard locations. These may be places we have visited, travelled through, or where we spent our childhood. Such locations can add depth and vision to later manuscripts.

4. Tidbits: some writers keep a junk file filled with tidbits they store just because they like the turn of a phrase or an unusual fact they may want to use someday.

Ideas are like rabbits. You get a couple and learn how to handle them, and pretty soon you have a dozen. (John Steinbeck)

WRITE WHAT IS IN THE IMAGINATIVE MIND

Write it down. We are writers. We are not just thinkers. Write it down. Buy a journal if that helps.

We write it on paper if it's in our minds. It may become a necessary detail for a future story or it may be fodder for the cyberbit recycling bin for reuse at a later time. It may be a turning point for a character we hadn't recognized or planned for. It may need to be cut and saved in our idea file, or it may only be garbage fit for final disposal.

No writing is wasted, even if it becomes nothing more than an exercise in learning what not to write.

It is a lot easier to cut during editing than try to remember what you were thinking two months ago.

OPENING PARAGRAPHS

Writing opening or first paragraphs can be a very handy skill or tool for multiple reasons. This can help us defeat the dreaded and dastardly blank page and get us started on actually writing. It energizes that literary genius toolbox between our ears. And sometimes, just sometimes, it develops into a full blown book or even a series of books.

Practicing writing opening paragraphs is simply writing throwaway literature. Well, it is throw away as long as we don't let our mothers near our trashcans. She won't let us throw anything away. Trust me—you don't want some of this drivel hanging on your mother's refrigerator for the neighbors to see. Write them with the intention of discarding, throwing away, and relegating the cyber bits to everlasting cyber glory.

There is usually no long-term investment in these paragraphs—it's practice. They're not designed to begin any work based on an existing storyline. This is the equivalent of a child practicing piano scales. Scales are played to train the ear and give the fingers muscle memory. Scales aren't generally played for audiences.

We should be able to dash off a practice first paragraph within two minutes, relative to typing speed. Practice is a matter of going to our writing toolbox and making sure all the tools we have are sharp, clean and ready to be put to use.

It's not necessary to pick a genre or a point of view. In fact, it's often beneficial to practice what we're not good at writing. Practice writing opening paragraphs for genres outside of your normal reading habits.

Our goal is to put something on paper that inspires a reader to continue reading. This isn't the journalism school of opening paragraphs that provides who, what, where, when, why and how. Why would readers need to finish the book if you tell them everything there is to know in the first paragraph? It's about laying out the foundation for our book's first literary hook.

Putting this in fishing terms, we are casting a lure. Most of the time, the fish won't strike. We reel in our line and cast again. Most practice paragraphs stink and should go to the garbage disposal as quickly as possible or the blank page will use it against us. Blank pages are mean that way and not above hitting below the belt.

This temporary opening paragraph should include a character, an activity, and a lure. Hidden in the lure is a hook. The hook may not be set deeply enough to catch a reader until later in the second, third, or even fifth paragraph. We're not interested in setting the hook. Our goal with practice paragraphs is to cast the lure, it doesn't need to strike water. Casting repeatedly is part of the fun.

WRITING PRACTICE FIRST PARAGRAPHS EXERCISE

Write between three to five sentences only for this exercise. In reality, opening paragraphs are not limited to three to five sentences in length. They may be much longer or much, much shorter. This is practice, not a sprint, or a marathon. Examples:

"Bob ran across the airfield. The danger wasn't from the huge aircraft landing and taking off, but from the gunmen chasing him. Everything around him seemed to be moving faster than he could run."

"Ginger grabbed Scooter's butt. It wasn't the most appropriate way to greet a stranger, but she was new to the singles dating scene. Besides, Grandma always said if you see what you want, you should grab it with both hands and hang on."

"Betty went with her mother to the store. She had been to the store before, but today was different. It would be just Mother and her. The twins were staying at Dad's for the weekend."

"Veronica stood in the street, letting the cold, winter rain splash mud onto her dress. The rain washed away the tears from her eyes as she stared at Cal's body lying bloody in the mud. The Harland boys had shot Cal and left him to bleed to death, and no one in the town of Peaceful, Arizona would help her move the body."

Note: I pounded out this practice paragraph in under a minute. It was originally written as—no surprise—a western. I liked it so much I turned it into a full-length novel. It became a science fiction manuscript, unpublished at this time, *A Planet with No Name.*

Now it's your turn to try your hand at writing five separate opening paragraphs. Remember to keep them between three and five sentences in length.

As we practice writing opening paragraphs, we should not throw away all of our practice. Put them in our story idea file. Here are some examples of the type of opening paragraphs practice to keep:
- We may just like the way a practice paragraph reads.
- We may have stumbled upon a clever turn of phrase.
- It sparks an idea for a story.
- We just like the way it smells. (Do I smell perfumed ink or burning cyber bits?)

Jot down a few notes on our story idea so ten years from now when we're searching for a story idea for that eighth, tenth or fourteenth novel, we will not forget what we were originally thinking.

READING FIRST PARAGRAPHS EXERCISE

Grab a stack of at least five books from your shelf of favorite reads. Choose them without regard to literary merit, genre or even the color of the book cover. Read just the first paragraph, nothing else, just the first paragraph.

- What elements do we see?
- What do we notice is not there? Look for who, what, where, when, why, and how.
- How did the author lure us in? What is that hook that makes us want to keep reading?

2.2 BASICS

WRITING IS DIFFICULT WORK

Only two to three percent of all manuscripts for novels are ever finished. This isn't said to convince you to quit. I say this because when we finish our book, we'll have beaten ninety-eight percent of everyone else. And frankly, if I can talk you out of writing another bad book, then I have done a good thing. Writing to completion will take dedication and commitment. Don't start if you aren't prepared to work at it.

Writing is a lifetime of hard work.

Be prepared to write a bad first draft.

A rough first draft is the first and primary goal. Bad writing leads to good writing. No one is good at their first attempt at anything with the exception of a few savants. This holds true for playing the violin, dancing the tango, making pancakes, and writing.

As many of us know, there is a vast difference between a five-year-old's first piano recital and the same child's recital after practicing for fifteen years. Many of us are still trying to make the perfect pancake. The point isn't to give up writing, but to expect that our first few attempts may not be as good as *To Kill a Mockingbird* by Harper Lee, *In Cold Blood* by Truman Capote, or *Gone with the Wind* by Margaret Mitchell. That isn't to say your first novel will be as bad as my first manuscript. You may indeed write the next best seller. It could happen.

That doesn't mean what we write has no merit, it just means that our second book will rock the world. But, we cannot write our second book until we get our first one yanked out of our imaginations, our minds, our brains and put on paper, or in the case of e-readers, put digitally into cyberspace in a relatively readable and logical order.

The primary benefit of completing our first draft is our own sense of accomplishment. An added benefit is to make our story available for our audience.

We don't want our readers amazed at our literary talent. We want our readers amazed they missed sleep because they couldn't put down our book. We want our readers amazed we made them laugh on one page and cry on the next. Save the fancy literary skills for a later rewrite.

Write one book at a time. This is specific advice for finishing our first manuscript. Remember: we have to write the whole story, not just snippets, scraps, bits and pieces, or oddments. Don't toss the leftovers out. Save them for later consumption. They don't belong on the table for our first literary feast. We need to keep what limited writing time we have available simple, sharp, and focused on finishing our first work.

There is no perfect topic. There is no perfect plotline, no perfect location, no perfect character, just as there are no perfect cars, perfect spouses—sorry, honey—or perfect day jobs. Forget about looking for perfection, writing our first draft is all about making mistakes. We can't make a mistake if we don't first write something.

Once we have a one-sentence summary we love, we can convert it into a novel. One sentence becomes one paragraph. We add a second sentence and a third to explain what, why, or the how of our first sentence. Need more explanation? Write a couple more sentences. A few sentences make a paragraph. Adding a few paragraphs to explain our first paragraph will make a page. A few pages become a chapter. Enough chapters and we have the manuscript of a novel.

This is the beginning of a story outline, but, our practice is just one little sentence. We can write one sentence, right? It's not a problem.

Don't wait for that flash of inspiration. We do not wait until that little voice inside our head gives us the word-for-word byplay of the next great novel. It usually doesn't work that way. Every fiction work goes onto paper the same way, one word at a time. Write one word and then write another.

ONE SENTENCE SUMMARY EXERCISE

Write a one-sentence summary of your proposed novel.

PLOT

As we write, we try to remember the six Cs of a good story: Crisis, Conflict, Characters, Contradiction, Controversy, and Conversation. That is why we read novels about knights and warriors, not about scribes and cobblers. Even character driven stories require these elements. A plot is no more than a list of actions and consequences.

This is a brief definition of each of the Cs. They are discussed more at length elsewhere in this book.

- Crisis - Revealing a situation, a period of uncertainty, difficulty, or even physical pain that has beset our main character; especially at a time when action is required to avoid disaster or the loss of everything. This is the turning point.
- Conflict - Opposition between forces or characters that controls the actions of our protagonist and antagonist.
- Characters - The protagonists and antagonists who inhabit our stories.
- Contradiction - Something that appears illogical or inconsistent that our protagonist must struggle in understanding.
- Controversy - Strong disagreement between our characters with both sides believing they're right.
- Conversation - Getting our characters to talk, whether it is casual, informal, contentious, or outright lies.

Here is a suggested sequence of events:
1. Introduction - We meet our protagonist in their normal surroundings.
2. Unforeseen event - Turning our hero's world upside down.
3. Goals - Give our characters goals. Achievement or failure is our option, but their struggle towards that goal will develop our plot. It doesn't matter if our main character wants these goals or they're forced upon them.
4. Imperfections - We find that our main character isn't perfect, but has blemishes and faults. Don't glob this all in at this time. Sprinkle it around.

5. Pursuit of the goal - Our protagonist must struggle to achieve the goal. Don't make it easy on them.
6. Unexpected successes - Our main character achieves some surprising rewards.
7. Crisis - Our protagonist is on the verge of failure.
8. Face-off - The last challenge with severe consequences, usually using what he has learned as he struggles toward the goal.
9. The End - The happily ever after (HEA) where everyone celebrates the hero achieving his goal or commiserating over his abject failure. It's our choice.

Be unique and unpredictable. We use our *what if* to twist our stories so that even we are surprised at the turn of events. We have a lock on a good story if we can surprise ourselves. Very few of us want to read a rehash of a bad television show. Unique means one of a kind. That may be impossible in the overall scheme of literature, but what we write with the basic storyline in our head will determine the uniqueness of our work.

The things I want to know are in books; my best friend is the man who'll get me a book I ain't read. (Abraham Lincoln)

Our plots are our foundation for a reader's understanding, entertainment, and appreciation. Our readers will be unhappy if they cannot follow from point A to point B and then to point C. We must build a strong foundation. A plot flaw is a bug in the matrix, a place where the record skips, a mental moment of brain freeze. Plots must have believable causes; otherwise our readers will stumble over the distractions.

Secondary Plots are common. Consider using them. We must force more than one set of actions on our characters. They won't like it, but they will be better for it in the long run. This helps us keep our stories from becoming one dimensional. We are more than one thing at one time. We are spouses, children, grandparents, employees, employers, chauffeurs, lovers, teachers, students, advisers, friends, and enemies. Each part of our life demands a separate plot line.

Develop your own style of writing: outlining versus seat of the pants. There are two basic types of writers. There are those who plot by writing outlines and then follow their outline step-by-step and there are those who just go with the flow, letting the story develop, seemingly on its own. This doesn't mean that we must be one or the other. Almost every writer will do a little of both and a mixture of each. We must all find our own comfort zone. We will learn as we write our first novel that our own style will come to light. Both methods have their benefits and drawbacks.

Plotting by outline:
1. Our direction is clear from beginning to end. This may speed us along to the ultimate goal of getting our story written.
2. We can write directly on a copy of our outline. We take the bullet point section, flesh it out and delete the outline point as we go and continue writing. This will give us a sense of accomplishment and we can judge how far along we are in the story.
3. Our work may feel contrived and predetermined as we struggle to keep our characters in line with that expected finish.

Seat of the pants:

1. Writers who use this method exclusively don't always know where the story is going. Consequently, the writer may lose his way and meander off into meaningless exposition. I refer to this as going tangental. This does not mean a tangent is bad writing. It may be very good, but if it doesn't move the story along or add depth and meaning to the story, it doesn't belong in our first novel.

2. Writers who use this method may receive unexpected results as their imagination catches fire, giving them the opportunity to write beyond an initial outline.

BRAINSTORMING IDEAS

Groups – talk to friends, family, or writers' groups. Good ideas flow from good conversations. This is where we need to excel in active listening. We learn to sprinkle conversations with open ended questions, eliciting more than a yes or no response. We learn to listen to the conversation and not force it to go where we want it to go. So much the better if our conversants aren't focused on helping us with our book, but just letting the conversation flow willy-nilly.

Remember to give credit where credit is due. You will want to enter in the book's acknowledgement section near the dedication, "Thanks to Cousin Billy-Bob for his hunting badgers at night insight".

Creativity is inventing, experimenting, growing, taking risks, breaking rules, making mistakes, and having fun. (Mary Lou Cook)

BORROW STORYLINES

I have read *Wuthering Heights* by Emilie Bronte rewritten as a western. I have read *The Count of Monte Cristo* by Alexandre Dumas as a Vietnam War era suspense thriller. Most of us have seen Shakespeare's *Romeo and Juliet* adapted as a musical movie. I have seen the great western *High Noon* re-done as a science fiction movie.

All we borrow is the storyline. That is nothing more than writing about a boy from this side of the tracks, meets a girl from that side of the tracks. Everybody objects and a fight— or musical dance number ensues. Either the couple dies or everyone lives happily ever after. That is our choice. We aren't borrowing points of view, characters, names, locations or even plot twists.

A good place to borrow a storyline is to read a book's back cover blurb. I'm constantly amazed that the back cover teaser doesn't take the novel in the direction I would have taken it or even bear any resemblance to what the book is about.

Many storylines are ancient and the author can't or won't object to their use. Shakespeare and Grimm's Fairy Tales are fair game. There are more diverse storylines hidden in the Bible than you'll find on most library shelves. For example, the David and Goliath storyline is in common usage. It's a cliché in sports stories precisely because the basic storyline works. It's how we treat the story, how we twist it and mold it to our vision that makes for a good read. What follows is an example of borrowing a storyline. Look at the story of Ruth and her mother-in-law Naomi.

Naomi goes with her husband to live in another land with her two sons due to a plague in their homeland. The sons marry women of the new land.

The men die … all of them. It is like, crap, this woman cannot catch a break. Naomi is broke and empty. She decides to return to her homeland.

Ruth begs to go with her.

Ruth says, "Intreat me not to leave thee, or to return from following after thee: for whither thou goest, I will go; and where thou lodgest, I will lodge: thy people shall be my people, and thy God my God: Where thou diest, will I die, and there will I be buried: the Lord do so to me, and more also, if ought but death part thee and me."

Back in Naomi's homeland a distant relative of Naomi's sees and helps Ruth. The kinsman marries Ruth and takes care of both Ruth and Naomi.

Now, let's make this storyline our own.

Natalie and her husband Ernie live with their two teenage sons in the little town of Nacogdoches, Texas. Ernie loses his job at an oil refinery. He moves Natalie and the boys to Los Angeles where he gets a job working on an oilrig in the Pacific. The boys grow, get jobs with Dad, and marry California girls, Randi and Glenda.

A freak accident causes an explosion, killing Ernie and the boys. Natalie feels lost, alone and empty in LA. It is a hard city to live in if you come from a small town. She decides to move back to Nacogdoches, Texas.

Randi—her late oldest son's wife—says, "You are my family. Please, please, please ask me to go and I will go. If you do not ask, I will follow you anyway. You have family there. They are my family now. The church you go to will be the church I go to. We will be roommates. If you die, then I will surely die as well for you are more my mother than my own mother ever was and only death will separate us."

Randi moves with her. Randi gets a job waiting tables and Natalie struggles to make ends meet as a cafeteria worker at the high school. Randi meets Bob, a second cousin of Ernie, who owns a car dealership. They get married and Natalie moves into the guesthouse out back on Bob and Randi's ranch to help raise her grandkids.

The author of the original story Ruth and Naomi story will not complain of plagiarism.

PLAGIARISM IS A NO-NO

Plagiarism is a no-no. Plagiarize means to steal another's words or literature. It means to not give credit where credit is due. It means to offer another's work as your own. It is fraud.

I would give an exact definition of literary plagiarism, but that would mean I would have to look it up. Then I would have to give credit to where I got the information.

When in doubt—leave it out. Do not use something if there is any question as to whether its use would constitute plagiarism or misuse of copyrighted material. Throw it out, start over or re-write it completely.

Our imaginations are flexible enough to generate our own twists on old stories.

2.3 WRITE WHAT WE KNOW AND WRITE WHAT WE READ

PERSONAL FOCUS
Focus on telling the story. Don't focus on the finish.

Pick a person to write for and stick to that personal focus. We write as if we're telling the story to just one person. Pick someone we know well enough to know how to keep his or her attention. Write for Mom, the spouse, a brother, or for crazy Uncle Herbert.

A writer only begins a book. A reader finishes it. (Samuel Johnson)

KNOW OUR AUDIENCE
Our audience is generally not genre neutral. They read what they enjoy reading, sometimes that keeps them within a specific genre. A construction worker may have the ability to read hard-core, technical, military science fiction, but they may prefer romance novels.

Science Fiction is no more written for scientists than ghost stories are written for ghosts. (Brian Aldiss)

You may write the great American novel. I will not. I don't have any desire to write it. I just want people to read my books and say, "Hey! Thanks. It made me forget about the mortgage payments for a few hours." That is my audience. If I were to send some of my work to my father, he would answer with a response reminiscent of how the days of the week look like if you remove Monday and Tuesday (W T F). For those stories, he isn't my audience.

Ask yourself these questions:
- Who is my audience?
- Who am I writing for?
- Who do I expect to read what I write?

SELECT A SPECIFIC GENRE

Selecting a specific genre provides a focused structure—familiar flavor—as we begin writing. This provides two specific and yet somewhat vague viewpoints:

1. Specific, because there are a limited number of genres available. This limitation is stretching even as we speak, because writers are constantly pushing the genre boundaries.
2. Vague, because it's our writing and we don't have to accept that same limitation. It's nobody's business if we mix our genres. Booksellers hate this because they don't know how to pigeonhole our work on their shelves. Right now, we're concerned with writing, not with marketing, so feel free to mix and match.

There are plenty of genres to choose from and many subgenres within each category. The following list isn't intended to be comprehensive, but to help us in selecting our ultimate destination. We should be as careful in genre selection as a drunk, blindfolded fratboy playing pin the tail on the donkey. We can choose to write any one or any mixture of the following:

- Action-Adventure
- Chick Lit
- Children's—up to middle grade
- Christian Fiction
- Ethnic—any work focused toward a specific culture
- Erotic

- Fantasy
- General Fiction—comedy, commercial, contemporary, literary, mainstream
- Historical
- Horror—paranormal, thriller
- Inspirational
- LGBT—Lesbian, Gay, Bisexual, Transgender
- Middle Grade
- Mystery—crime, detective, psychological, suspense, thriller
- New Adult
- Romance—comedy, contemporary, historical, paranormal, rural, or suspense
- Science Fiction—apocalyptical, hardcore, military, near earth, or space opera
- Sports
- Western
- Young Adult Fiction—can fit any genre or any age

We choose our genre because we are hampered by the old adage write what you know. This phrase is often vastly misunderstood. It would be better phrased write what you read. If we read westerns, we should write westerns. If we read romance novels, we should write romance novels. This doesn't mean we must understand quantum physics and warp drive theory to write science fiction.

Readers of specific genres have a deep understanding for what they read. There are genre conventions and rhythms. As writers, we will produce our most compelling work when we pay homage to these genre specific conventions and rhythms. That doesn't mean we can't write a romance novel with a sports theme or cloak our inspirational thriller in a science fiction cape of Hispanic manufacturing.

While I do harp on not having any rules as we are writing our first novel for ourselves, we should keep in mind that someday, somewhere, and at sometime, we may want to share our work. Who will read what we write? We run the risk of getting lost in the weeds if we stray too far from the pre-paved genre pathways.

We must read more than we write, even if we have to schedule the time to do it. We write what we read. Reading is the best way to determine our audience. We write for ourselves and we write for people who like to read the same literature we enjoy.

Every genre has a rhythm and a flow. Every sub-genre fits into that rhythm and flow, but with a few variations on the existing theme. The style may vary among authors, but the story has the same underlying feel to it.

Every genre uses its own language. A simplified example is the accepted meaning of words to regular readers of the genre. Pull the word gravity from your toolbox. Our readers will know we are writing about the mutual attraction between two bodies relative to mass if we are writing science fiction. We will not need to explain the meaning of the word to our readers. They will get it. Again, pull the word gravity from our toolbox. Our readers will know we are writing about the seriousness of the situation if we are writing a courtroom drama. Our readers will know without explaining it.

We write what we read. Many of us claim to read everything and anything we can get our hands on. That may be true. But what books do we keep on our shelf and what books go to the garage sale, used bookstore, or the charity book drive? Some of us actually do read and enjoy everything and anything. A clever and talented writer can mix genres successfully. I have picked up a science fiction book in the romance section of a bookstore and read about vampires.

Many writers can write different genre styles just as many musicians can play rock, country and classical. Most do not try to mix them together. A few successful writers will produce works in more than one genre. For example, Ian Fleming wrote the original James Bond spy series and the children's classic, *Chitty Chitty Bang Bang*.

It may feel overly simplistic, but we should pick specifics for our first novel.
- Pick a genre.
- Pick a point of view.
- Pick a conflict.

We should write what we want to know. This may be a challenge for a first book, but if we want to learn about ballroom dancing, try to incorporate ballroom dancing into our story. A note of caution: research time is not writing time. We can't take dance lessons at Arthur Astaire's Dance Studio and call it writing. It's research.

Alternately, we write what we do not know. We don't write about us. This is fiction, not an autobiography or a memoir. We may use real life events, but we must twist and turn them to be unrecognizable by anyone who was there. Remember real life can be stranger than fiction. Sometimes it's hard to believe what really happened.

We write what we want to write. Just poo-poo everyone who says we should write about this, or write about that, or write about both at the same time. Our task is to write. Our desire to write is prime.

We write the book we want to read. Would we pull this story off the bookshelf if we walked into a bookstore? Would we read the book if someone else wrote it?

We should assume our first book won't sell. We don't need the sales pressure at this point. Your first work might turn out to be the next best thing to *Great Expectations* by Charles Dickens, but that thought comes after all of the words have been wrangled into the corral in suitable order.

ADD WHAT DOES NOT BELONG
This is a tricky subject among writers. But remember, there are no rules we cannot break. Add romance to an action story. Add humor to a mystery novel. Add mystery to a romance book. We should stay within our genre, but a novel can be a long story. We can thread in a few additives to get our story firing on all cylinders.

Thus, in a real sense, I am constantly writing autobiography, but I have to turn it into fiction in order to give it credibility. (Katherine Paterson*)*

MAKE IT PERSONAL

This story is from our hearts. We care so we make the readers care. Write with all five senses. Smell what we write. Hear the wind in the clouds. See every note in the rhythm of our stories. If we touch our hearts and touch our character's hearts, then we will touch our reader's hearts.

Some books are to be tasted, others to be swallowed, and some few are to be chewed and digested... (Francis Bacon)

2.4 BUILD A FRAME

CHARACTERS

Readers become invested in the primary character within the first five paragraphs. Don't delay their introduction. Many crime drama writers like to start with the crime. It works on television because we have already been introduced to the stars and lead characters of the show. It doesn't work as well in literature where the story is written, not visual, certainly not for our all-important first book.

You take people, you put them on a journey, you give them peril, you find out who they really are. If there's any kind of fiction better than that, I don't know what it is. (Joss Whedon)

Do not introduce the main protagonist after ancillary characters.

Do not introduce the reader to a character who will not return later in the story. We don't need to know the cab driver's name or how many children he has unless it's integral to the storyline where the cab driver or his children make another or repeated appearances.

Always give the reader a hero. Don't tell everything about the main character up front. The hero may not be our primary character, especially if we are writing from the point of view of a psychopathic serial killer. But, our readers need someone to empathize with, to applaud and to cheer for when the psychopath is finally stopped.

Define the characters by physical attributes, such as age, height, hair color, eye color, and sex— not just male or female. Often sex means defining by sure, never, often, seldom, gay, or straight.

Define the characters by their major goal and why. Everybody wants something. What does this character want? What past events have affected this goal? What is the motivation for their actions? What are their pet peeves? Is the character's primary personality—grumpy, dopey, sleepy, happy, sneezy, bashful, or doc?

Only tell a reader what they absolutely must know at this point in the story to understand why the character does what he or she does. Characters change and grow. How is this character going to develop? A writer recently shared with me that she writes a journal for her main characters, written from the character's point of view. Why they did what they did and how they felt about it. This method may make your characters more real in your imagination enabling them to grow into more developed characters in your story.

Define the character with as much information as you can. Don't worry about shoving all this information into the story. It won't all fit, but what we do add in will add depth and richness to our story.

The more real our characters become to us, the more they will aid us in writing their story. Characters have no character aside from what we provide them and what we allow the reader to imagine. Readers imagine less than we think they will. Readers also imagine completely differently than we do. What is added and what is left out will give balance to a character.

We define characters completely for our own understanding, but we tell our readers only what they need to know. Don't force the character to do something they would not normally do. We designed their personality. If the action is something they must do, then we give them a reason to do it against their will. Trust me, those characters will love us if we motivate them.

It's okay to fall in love with our characters. We should always give our characters choices with the understanding there are consequences to every choice. Consequences can be good or bad.

We never end up with the book we began writing. Characters twist it and turn it until they get the life that is perfect for them. A good writer won't waste their time arguing with the characters they create...It is almost always a waste of time and people tend to stare when you do! (C.K. Webb)

No one is all bad. No one is all good. Most of us are a mixture of both. Our characters should have both good and bad character traits.

For example, let's say Madam Revere is the character. If we want her to become a homicidal lesbian dance instructor, that's our business. Conversely, we should be careful not to push her into becoming too much of a cliché. We must be careful with character development or she will be just like every other New York dance instructor since Shirley Temple put on tap shoes. Even a tertiary contact can alter the hero's life course; that is more true to life than most of us want to publically admit.

ONE SENTENCE CHARACTER SUMMARY EXERCISE

Write one sentence about a sympathetic protagonist, hero or good guy. This can be anyone from a twelve-year-old girl scout to a seventy-year-old ex-convict. This can be anywhere from Smalltown, USA to a halfway house in the big city.

1. Write four good things the main character does. Try to stay within the realm of positive activities: always stops to pet kittens, helps old ladies with their groceries, gives a hungry puppy half her sandwich, or volunteers to give blood.
2. Write two character flaws or bad habits in the main character's personality. No one is perfect. Neither is any protagonist. Will he sleep with anything in a skirt? Does she put off doing her homework until it's too late? Does he worry too much about things he cannot change. Does she like to fart in crowded elevators and then try to pass the blame off on some random fat guy? Character flaws add depth and realism to our characters.

Write one sentence about an antagonist or bad guy. This can be anyone from a twelve-year-old spoiled boy to a thirty-year-old ex-addict. It can be anywhere from Richtown, USA to living on the streets.

1. Write four negative character attributes this adversary has.
2. Write two positive things or good habits attributed to this bad guy. This can be helpful to a good story as good habits help the writer literarily hide the bad guy until it is too late.

DESCRIPTIONS

State early if the heroine is a redhead, but only if it is important to the storyline in chapter five. Otherwise, don't tell the reader. Readers will fill in a lot of information as they read. Only tell a reader what they have to know about how the character looks. The reader's imagination will fill in the blanks.

Avoid cliché character descriptions. For example, tall willowy redheads are much more common in science fiction and western stories than they are in real life.

Do not explain or describe everything. Writing everything about a subject or activity can be as boring and time consuming as reading through pages of technical specifications explaining why the mass spectrometer isn't giving the correct reading needed to solve the crime. Most readers don't care how the microwave works, just that it does. Writing more than necessary is like that whole chapter in *Moby Dick* where Herman Melville describes whaling. A modern reader just doesn't need to know that much about it.

Readers have imaginations of their own. As writers, our whole job is to give our readers an operational framework for their imaginations. Children are much happier playing inside a fenced area than in an open field. It gives them boundaries. My brothers and I were always content to play on our grandparent's farm as children. Grandpa always said, "You can go anywhere on the place you want to go, just don't cross any fences." Our job as writers is to build those fences.

It isn't our job to describe every leaf and the alignment of every rock. Sure, there are leaves and sure there are rocks.

Toss in a few cows and a mean Shetland pony and we'll have a perfect place for an imagination to run wild.

I once met a literary agent who quoted the old hairy-legged cliché—the devil is in the details. That would be fine if we want to dance with the devil. We do not. We lay out the canvas, brushes, and paints with our words, allowing our readers to paint the final picture.

Only write enough information about weather to get the characters reaction to it. "Mary was cold." That tells us what we need to know. We do not need to muddle through a chapter on the wind chill index and the varying degrees of cold. Mary was cold, so what did she do? The action taken is the important part of the story.

It begins with a character, usually, and once he stands up on his feet and begins to move, all I can do is trot along behind him with a paper and pencil trying to keep up long enough to put down what he says and does. (William Faulkner)

PRIMARY CHARACTERS
This is our protagonist. This may or may not be the hero of the story. This is the focal character and their actions and reactions drive the story forward.

Our primary character may be giving voice to our story or it may be about them. This is our most defined character. That doesn't mean we provide an immediate detailed description of this character down to the mole on the back of their left knee. We must ensure the reader knows about the character's physical, mental, and emotional boundaries, about the restrictions and limitations that drive and determine their actions. Why do they do what they do? Why did they react the way they did?

We are not required to explain this at the character's first appearance. Give the reader the courtesy of getting to know the primary character. Let the character grow and progress. Let them breathe a while. Readers will learn to love or hate our primary character as our story progresses. The primary characters may grow or decline throughout the length of our story.

Plan to add primary character flaws. No one is all bad or all good. Even sociopaths will pet a friendly dog and a psychopath will open the door for a pregnant woman. Allow the protagonist to be afraid of heights, spiders, or even snakes. Flaws can drive a person's actions. For example, in my novel *Metal Boxes*, my primary character grew up in space ships and on space stations. He had a fear of open spaces. Defining that flaw helped develop the story and gave depth to the character.

Establish the primary character's moral imperatives. There are some things people will not do, no matter what the situation. These may not be spelled out in our story, but we should know this about the character. Moral imperatives are stumbling blocks that our characters deal with in their struggles through our pages.

Alternately, there are things our primary character must do, no matter what the situation. Some people must stop and get the puppy off the freeway, no matter how fast the traffic, no matter the possible cost to their life, no matter how ugly the puppy.

Avoid stereotypes. Stereotypes are a lot like clichés except they are more generally applied. I won't go into these. You know what they are.

Our protagonist moves the story, not us. This is difficult for many new writers to understand. Characters move from step to step. Sure, the writing moves their feet, but they live through the story; we're just telling it.

SECONDARY CHARACTERS

These are the people who inhabit the primary character's world. They are not as well defined as the primary character. They only need to be motivationally apparent and activity oriented. Why did they do what they did? As writers, we need to be cognizant of their actions only concerning how those actions have any effect on our story.

Basic descriptions are all that are required, unless it is necessary to the storyline. When we introduce Sam into the storyline in chapter three the reader will build a mental image of Sam around the given character descriptions. It will severely damage the flow of the story if, in chapter eighteen, Sam couldn't climb the wall to help the primary character because Sam is too fat. The reader's mental image of Sam won't match his later actions if we didn't tell our readers that Sam is fat in chapter three during that first introduction.

We don't always have access to our secondary characters innermost thoughts, feelings, hopes and dreams. If those innermost thoughts, feelings, hopes, and dreams have an impact on our primary character, we must ask our secondary character to speak up. If they will not talk to the primary character—and some characters are shy that way—they will need to speak to someone else so the primary character can somehow learn about it.

These characters are a contrast to the protagonist. Their most apparent purpose is to provide a backdrop allowing our lead character to shine. Dr. Watson was smart, but his intelligence showed how exceptionally smart Sherlock Holmes was in comparison.

Secondary characters often provide key information that our protagonist may not have any other way to learn. Think about the lab tech in a police drama or the bartender in a western novel.

Secondary characters provide us access to backstory. This isn't a flashback, but this type of character may be a sister, brother or childhood friend. Their contributions to dialog and conversations can give us the reasons why our protagonist does what he does. For example:
- "Mom always said you were a bit of a fussbudget."
- "Remember how your dad tanned your hide when you broke Mr. Hanson's window?"
- "That waitress looks like the girl you took to the prom. What was her name?"

Secondary characters provide a sounding board for the protagonist. They are someone the primary character can talk to as they work through solutions to a problem. This type of secondary character keeps our readers out of our lead character's head. There is only so much patience a reader has for sentences like:
- "John thought..."
- "John imagined..."
- "John considered..."

John needs someone to talk to even if it's a mangy old dog who doesn't talk back.

Secondary characters contribute to conflict, both minor and major. Our protagonist will go to war with or for these characters. Some are so trouble-prone that our lead character spends much of his life getting his good buddy out of trouble.

They serve as red-herrings in mysteries, suspense and thrillers. A red herring is the character the reader believes to be the most likely suspect ... until he isn't. They can be a focal point for clues, hints and revealed secrets, yet they are as innocent as they have always professed to be ... or not.

Every character should want something, even if it is only a glass of water. (Kurt Vonnegut)

TERTIARY CHARACTERS
They are cannon fodder. They appear and disappear like extras in the movies. The reader is aware of their existence, but they do not impact our reader's hearts or the heart of our primary character.

Kill them off if you desire or allow them to wander around leading useless, boring little lives, without ever knowing what they missed out on being in our new literary work. It is much kinder to kill them off quickly than to allow them to discover we wrote about them. Sometimes these tertiary characters only deserve a passing mention in a quick sentence that may end up in the trash or being assigned to—wherever cyber bits go when you delete them.

These characters are often known as *red shirts* in science fiction. Their whole lot in life is to die while giving our protagonist motivation, clues, and emotional or mental pegs.

Emotional or Mental Pegs are those reminders humans use to stimulate emotions. A song is an emotional peg when it reminds us of an incident, accident or an individual. A smell is a strong emotional peg reminding us of Aunt Peg who wore the same fragrance. The way something feels or tastes can stimulate memory. Our tertiary characters often act as emotional or mental pegs for our primary characters. For example: "That girl looks like MaryBeth. I need to call her." Or "That girl looks like MaryBeth. She broke my heart and I won't ever let that happen again." Why would our main character want to remember MaryBeth (or Aunt Peg, for that matter)? That's for us, the writer, to decide.

Try to avoid giving names to tertiary characters. Farmers don't name the chicken they're having for Sunday dinner. These characters don't deserve any physical description beyond what's necessary to explain their existence and their impact, if any, on our primary and secondary characters.

ABSENT CHARACTERS
Someone who is discussed but never seen. This is the captain of a ship, the pilot of a plane, or God. They can only be used when their actions or inactions affect the storyline through our protagonist, either directly or indirectly.

An example of this would be the story of a teenage boy raised in a strong matriarchal family. His grandmother ruled the home, although both parents were with him. As he moves along the plot line in our story he is constantly driven by the strength of his grandma's character. Such as:

- "Grandma says…"
- "Grandma would never allow…"
- "Grandma does it…"

Fully developing Grandma's character allows us to add depth and motivation to our teenager's actions. He has learned to do what he does at his grandma's knee. We, as the writer, will understand him because we know more about Grandma. Will he do what Grandma would say to do or in typical teenage rebellion, do just the opposite? We should know why he is doing what he is doing. Was Grandma a tyrant, a benevolent dictator, or a loving leader? Even though Grandma never graces the pages of our book, she has a lasting impression on our young teenage boy. Grandma will make an impression on our readers through the young boy.

Write Grandma's character off to the side as a reference for her actions. Do not insert it into the story.

CHARACTER NAMES
Character names need only be ethnically derived if it is germane to the storyline. However, there is no reason not to have an Irishman named Garcia if you so desire. You don't even need to explain why. It just is.

Do not waste time on character names beyond what specifically is necessary to story flow and rhythm. Where can you draw names? They come from anywhere and everywhere.

I often select the name of someone I know. Trust me, most people will be honored to be represented in our literary efforts. This doesn't hold true if you name the bad guy after them. If we need a name for our bad guy, use the name of someone we don't like.

If I am really stumped for a specific name, I will drop a movie into the player and go to the credits at the end. I chose a last name at random. The next person on the list provides a first name. Switch the names if you want to really irritate the character; last name first and first name last. For example; from the movie *High Noon* I can give a character the name 'Hayward Chubby'. The character is defined by the name alone. More examples from the same movie could be:
- Reed Syd
- Philip Lucien
- Mac James
- London Merrill
- John Nolan
- Graham Thomas

These are all good unless we are seeking an ethnically diverse name. If that is the case, we pick an ethnically diverse movie and be imaginative. It should be fun.

Other places to pull names from is a phone book or an internet baby name site. Keep a file listing of good names.

Keep an easy to use cast of characters list specific to this first novel. Make it an expandable list adding details as we write. This will help us with continuity on recurring characters, character growth as the story progresses, and proper spelling of their names.

Reading gives us someplace to go when we have to stay where we are. (Mason Cooley)

LOCATION
Set this from the beginning. By set, I don't mean to just throw a dart at a map. Come to an understanding of the location, its people, its culture and its oddities. When I say set, I mean S.E.T.

Select (S)
The setting must be appropriate to the storyline. Sometimes the best stories about Ohio farmers are when they aren't in Ohio. If we're going to write a fish out of water story, we need to have the water clear enough we can watch the fish.

Envision (E)
We need to have a clear mental picture in our imagination of our literary location. It isn't necessary to go to Brazil to get a clear vision or to spend hours researching the country. It might be enough for our purposes to know tulips and windmills are from Holland, not Norway. If we can see it in our imagination, then our readers will see it as they read.

Tease (T)
We don't tell our readers everything we know about Mudsuck, West Virginia. We try to give our readers just enough information to build a framework for our characters, to paint a picture in the reader's mind. We give them enough information so they will be tempted to go to West Virginia just to see the place. We show them a glimpse behind the curtain, but not enough to give them a good look.

Location affects our story almost as much as characters do and will have an important impact on our characters. We must remember—this is fiction. We make up what we do not know. Most of our readers will forgive us if there is no Fifth Street in Fredonia, Kansas and we say there is. Most of our readers will not forgive us if our character lives in

Fredonia, Kansas and we have him spending the time between work and supper waxing his surfboard. "Surf's up!" is not a phrase heard in Kansas unless our character needs his lithium dosage adjusted.

People from Minnesota are much different from those who live in Arizona. Is our main character a Maine character, but he lives in Tokyo? We need to understand how people in Tokyo act, to understand how they react to our Maine character and how our character interacts with them. We need to understand the regional idiosyncrasies that make Mainers different.

Cultural differences based on a locational backstory can add conflict and personality clashes to our storyline. Much of what we determine from our location notes may never make it into our story. But it will affect how our character acts and what motivates him.

Regional issues include weather oddities driven by terrain. Are we having tornadoes in Fairbanks, Alaska? Probably not. However, as we all know, we can have tornadoes in a trailer park in Oklahoma. Floods, earthquakes, forest fires or hurricanes all add to the depth of our location even if they don't impact our characters in a significant way. Rain in Seattle? Yep! Probably gonna happen. Sunny day in San Diego? Yassir! Don't see any reason today would be different than yesterday. Bodacious day in Texas? Well, if you say so.

Keep a map of your location. Print out a state road map of Alabama or use a hand drawn diagram of the mall showing what store goes where. It helps with a character's sense of direction and spatial awareness. Make sure the coffee shop doesn't mysteriously move from one spot to the next, if the story takes place in the mall. Remember: maps are flat; towns are not.

What is the history of our chosen location? True history can sometimes be hard to discern, but when in doubt go with the myth. We should know the history. Small quick asides or inside comments can tease and taunt a reader enough to do a search to see if such a place is real. For example, *The Friendship Stones* takes place near Oasis, Missouri. The town doesn't exist on any map, but it once did. It was buried under Table Rock Lake as the waters backed up. My grandmother remembered the town before they built the dam and scuba divers now tour its remains. My brother says the place is a myth, but then he never listened to Grandma anyway.

What is the political climate of our chosen location? Is there political turmoil? Such a thing may not impact our plot, but brief comments will certainly add depth to a town. Our character may walk past a political rally and ignore it. He may pick up and throw away a campaign sign from his front yard; doing so in passing without any reference other than he wouldn't vote for that fat idiot no matter how pretty his wife is.

CONVERSATION
Conversation personalizes the story for the listener.

Move the story forward by the conversations, not by exposition. Your story is about people. People move the story. Example:
> 'Bob and Nancy went to the store to get a loaf of bread.'
> That is as dry and dull as the toast Bob is going to make from the bread.

Conversation enhances our story, helping us write more and write quickly. It allows our characters to speak to the reader and gives our characters an opportunity to reveal pieces of their motivation and their personality. Example:

Nancy said, "Bob, let's go to the store."

"Why? I'm in the middle of this game on TV," Bob replied.

"Because I need a loaf of bread."

"But you don't need me to carry a loaf of bread. Come on, woman. It can only weigh a pound or so."

Nancy said, "Yes, Bob. But, it's Sunday. I love you and want to spend the day with you, not watching you watch television. Besides, we can have sex in the produce section again if you go with me."

Bob was out the door, had the car running, and was ready to get the loaf of bread before Nancy could put on her coat.

Now we're talking bread pudding with rum sauce, not just a loaf of bread.

Do not start the book or a chapter with conversation. This isn't a hard and fast rule. However, it makes reading difficult. When this happens, the reader doesn't have an introductory frame of reference in their minds. Who is talking? Who are they talking to? What does their voice sound like?

Always write conversations for character. This doesn't mean that we write an accent. Accents are too hard to read and they break the rhythm and flow of our story. Write the local dialect by words. It's a *cellar* in New York and a *basement* in Missouri. It's *pop or Coke* on the East Coast and *soda* in the Midwest. It's a *hog* to the farmer, a *porcine* to the college professor and *bacon-on-the-hoof* to the foodie.

Separate characters by linguistic differences. A classic example is in the 1969 movie version of *True Grit*. Kim Darby's character never used contractions. John Wayne's character used contractions until the end when young Mattie's life began to have a redeeming effect on old Rooster Cogburn. Of course, this is a silly example, in a movie, no one will ever confuse Kim Darby with John Wayne. But, it does illustrate a simple method of character differentiation. A primary character will always speak in the same manner. Secondary characters each have their own manner of speech.

Far too many writers give their characters a chance to speak in monologues, to finish a whole thought, and to get their ideas across without the conversation diverting off topic. Real conversations don't work that way. Monologues died with Shakespeare. Leave them dead. Most people cannot finish a sentence before they are interrupted. Finishing a complete thought and getting a point across takes perseverance on the character's part.

Allow conversations to flow. Guide the direction of conversations, but don't force it. Sometimes conversations will move the story in a direction other than what we intended. Just like Bob and Nancy's trip to the store for a loaf of bread.

A writer — and, I believe, generally all persons — must think that whatever happens to him or her is a resource. All things have been given to us for a purpose, and an artist must feel this more intensely. All that happens to us, including our humiliations, our misfortunes, our embarrassments, all is given to us as raw material, as clay, so that we may shape our art. (Jorge Luis Borges*)*

Write conversation at cross-purposes. Try having a conversation where two people are not talking about the same thing. This isn't as difficult as most new writers imagine, especially conversations between characters that don't know each other well. Think about conversations a person might have on a first date. They spend as much time explaining what they mean as they do saying it in the first place.

Write for oblique responses. Not everyone will give a complete and honest answer to any question.

Avoid unnecessary dialogue. Delete any conversation that doesn't move the story forward. It may be a funny, well-written conversation, but we are writing a novel. Save it in the story file if it's really good. There may be a use for it in that next novel or the one after that.

Dialogue is he said / she said or he asked / she asked. Skip the rest. We do not need a lot of "Josh spoke with fire and determination in his voice as he yelled across…" Write the fire and determination in the conversation, not in the he said action tag portion of the sentence.

Have your characters argue. We don't need to know the outcome until the argument is over.

Conversation is imperative to good storytelling. Conversation personalizes the story for the listener.

2.5 NEVER END A WRITING SESSION UNLESS OUR PROTAGONIST IS IN TROUBLE

Never end a writing session unless our hero is in trouble. It keeps us writing and it keeps our reader interested enough to miss bedtime by another hour, or three, or stay up until 4:47 a.m. because they couldn't put the book down.

To set a forest on fire, you light a match. To set a character on fire, you put him in conflict. (James N. Frey)

CONFLICT
Even character driven stories require this element.

Conflict may arise from small issues, but the consequences must be deemed large. An average reader may say, "So what? I lied to my girlfriend last week. It ain't that big of a deal." The incident may be small, but to the character, the result must be devastating. Here are two examples:
* My girlfriend just died and the last thing I said to her was a lie.
* I lied to my wife and she made life changing decisions based upon that lie.

Conflict can be both internal and external. Conflict isn't just war and strife. Conflict can be tension, stress, and emotional turmoil. Internal conflict takes place in a person's mind. For example, it can be a struggle to make a decision or overcome a feeling. Internal conflicts are Man versus Self. External conflict generally takes place between a character and someone or something else, such as nature, another person(s), or an event or situation. External conflicts may be Man versus Man, Nature, or Society.

Key Conflict Tidbits
Both sides in a conflict have choices. Make an effort for both sides of a conflict to have options. The more options the more believable the story.

Never give everything away, it heightens the tension. Save the major conflict resolution for the final climax. Intensify the conflict as the book progresses.

Get progressively nastier with the protagonist. They will not thank us for it, but our reader will.

Try for the surprise. "I didn't see that coming". We try to surprise ourselves.

Write high-stakes conflicts. Trivial conflicts generate trivial stories.

Stories are not *about* conflict and action. Stories *are* conflict and action.

Give our characters goals to achieve. Make them struggle to reach or fail to reach that goal.

POTENTIAL CONFLICT VARIETIES
Conflict is what drives the characters to action, either the internal emotional turmoil or the external forces pushing at them. It's what keeps our readers reading to see if our hero wins or loses. I have not listed every possible conflict variety here, just a few that exist at this time.

Internal Conflict
Many literary critics consider man's internal turmoil, the man's personal growth and redemption, the highest form of

conflict. This is the classic Man versus Self conflict scenario.

Man versus Self. This is a conflict of a man's internal struggles to a resolution. It can be as devastating as a struggle against drug addiction or as common as a teenage boy's fear of calling a girl on the phone. Remember, it is the consequences of losing the struggle that provides the conflict.

Morality and desire fall into this type of conflict. To be a good character, he or she must have an internal conflict. Because we all have this, it's easy to write and be believable.

The greatest conflicts are not between two people but between one person and himself. (Garth Brooks)

External Conflict

Man versus Man. This is the conflict between two characters or between two groups of characters. It is the most common external conflict, and as such, it's one of the easiest to write. We and our readers can empathize with both sides of the conflict. This is the hero versus the villain.

Man versus Fate or Destiny. In this conflict, naming fate as the antagonist is a useful tool. Think *Oedipus Rex* by Sophocles. Consciously or unconsciously characters follow their fate.

Man versus Alternate Intelligence. This is a conflict between man and God, between man and aliens, or between man and an intelligent machine.

Man versus Society. This drives a character into conflict with governments, institutions, laws, culture or corrupt society. Think of *Divergent* by Veronica Roth or *The Hunger Games* by Suzanne Collins.

Man versus Supernatural. This is conflict driven by creatures of nightmares. Think of *Frankenstein* by Mary Shelley.

Man versus Technology. This conflict doesn't require an Alternate Intelligence. An excellent example is *Brave New World* by Aldous Huxley.

Man versus Nature. Nature can be a harsh antagonist. Personification can be used to twist nature into the protagonist.

Man versus Animal. This is a simple conflict. The animal can be the protagonist. Here we use the figure of speech personification or anthropomorphism, because it's difficult for our reader to empathize with the animal unless we give it specific human characteristics to draw the reader in.

Animal versus Animal. A common theme in children's books. Extreme personification must be used. *Aesop's Fables* is an excellent example.

Animal versus Nature. Think of Jack London's *Call of the Wild*.

Nature versus Nature. Really? I guess it is possible, but I don't recommend it for a first novel.

These conflicts can also be written backwards. For example: Alternate Intelligence (AI) versus Man where the AI is the protagonist and man is the antagonist.

CONFLICT FLOW
Uber

This conflict is the overreaching conflict taking many sequels to reach resolution. Example: a long storyline such as a master spy out to defeat an evil organized crime cartel. This will not be resolved in one book—it can lead to a long series or may never end.

Major

Major conflict must begin no later than paragraph five; the sooner the better. This is the book's primary conflict, it occurs within the confines of one work. Example: a cowboy's first cattle drive. It isn't his whole career as a bovine behavior modification specialist.

Sub

These are subplots. Example: the football player's on-going issue with the equipment manager and his on again-off again relationship with that tramp of a girlfriend. It isn't the major issue of winning the championship game, but the smaller issues that swirl around it.

Minor

Example: the argument the primary character has with any tertiary characters, or when she is trying to decide what color dress to wear.

How uber, major, sub and minor conflicts twist and intertwine is what makes masterful story telling. There should be instances where more than one conflict intersects in our story. These are the crossroads, the crux, and the crisis that drive our protagonist into action.

CONFLICT RESOLUTION
We can end our story as long as our protagonist reaches a comfortable, long-term resting point and has achieved or failed to achieve a stated goal. This school of thought allows us to move easily to a sequel. Not everything in life is wrapped up in a neat little bow. There are loose ends to everything in life.

The second school of thought on conflict resolution requires the writer to tie up all loose ends. Readers already live life. Many readers devour books to escape life, to live vicariously through another's life, or to experience something new. They don't need another frustration in their lives. Tell them what happened.

2.6 MAKE BAD THINGS HAPPEN TO OUR CHARACTERS

TROUBLE ABOUNDS

Never end a writing session unless the protagonist, the heroine, that literary good buddy, is in trouble. In writing, this is known as a hook. In the movies, they call it a cliffhanger. This is an effective writing tool to drive us back to writing as much as it is a tool to keep our reader's noses in the book.

If you want to write a fantasy story with Norse gods, sentient robots, and telepathic dinosaurs, you can do just that. Want to throw in a vampire and a lesbian unicorn while you're at it? Go ahead. Nothing's off limits. But the endless possibility of the genre is a trap. It's easy to get distracted by the glittering props available to you and forget what you're supposed to be doing: telling a good story. Don't get me wrong, magic is cool. But a nervous mother singing to her child at night while something moves quietly through the dark outside her house? That's a story. Handled properly, it's more dramatic than any apocalypse or goblin army could ever be. (Patrick Rothfuss)

Hooks are subtle and sometimes not so subtle literary devices that keep a reader involved in the story. They keep the reader reading to find out why, who, what or even, huh? Hooks may be the hint of danger on the wings of perfume drifting on the air or an in-your-face serial killer in your bedroom. They can be action oriented with the hero literally hanging off a cliff, or depending on what you're writing, they can be emotional cliffhangers. Example: "Why did she snub me at work if she really loves me?"

Every reader has needed to stop reading to get something else done. Everyone has said, "I will stop at the end of this chapter." But, when the end of the chapter arrives they can't quit. They must keep reading, continuing to look for a good place to stop. When that happens, we have written a good hook.

Writers can employ the same device, the hook, in our daily writing activities. We have pulled a character from our imagination, from our past, from our present lives or our hoped for future. We care about and have compassion for our literary friend. We cannot help but push ourselves back to the typewriter, computer, or Big Chief Tablet if, at the end of each writing session, we have left our protagonist stuck in a dreadful fix. We like them and want them safe, healthy, and emotionally stable, so we work to make them so. With enough good hooks in a book, an author can keep their readers up until 3 a.m.

Caution: we are rambling aimlessly in our writing if we have been processing words for a while and our hero isn't in trouble.

HOOKS
The first and most important hook must be set within the first five paragraphs of your story, sooner if possible. That is why we practice writing first paragraphs.

Hooks deal with who, what, where, when, why and how. Adding hooks in odd places is how we make our story flow.

Hooks never need explanation. The story drives the hook, not the other way around. A hook ties two pieces of our story together. Do not bait a hook and cast it into the water without a connection to the second piece. How far we cast that hook into the story's waters is up to us, the writer. However, don't frustrate the reader too long or they will give up.

Empathy as a hook. Hooks are not always action oriented. Emotional hooks can sink in deep. Meaningful struggles help a reader connect with the story, so hooks need to be within the scope of our reader's emotional subset. We try to make ourselves cry, or become angry, or feel protective. If we can feel this way when writing it, our readers will feel it, too.

TROUBLE IS WHAT FICTION IS ALL ABOUT

Develop a loveable character and then do every nasty thing to them we can think of. This is what we do. First we get them into trouble, then our job is to fix their problems, from winning the girl to reaching the peak of Mount Everest, from overcoming teen angst to defeating addiction, and from saving a cat in a tree to single-handedly taking down a terrorist cell.

Write what disturbs you, what you fear, what you have not been willing to speak about. Be willing to be split open. (Natalie Goldberg)

Hooks are baited with the troubles of our protagonist. Our stories progress as a series of troubles and fixes: trouble, trouble, fix, trouble, trouble fix, trouble, fix, trouble, fix, trouble, fix, fix, fix. Our readers will not quit reading if we can make our readers care as much about our protagonist as we do. Our hooks and cliffhangers keep us actively working to save our hero and make our readers sleepy the next day at work.

Best practice: never end a writing session unless our protagonist is in trouble.

CHAPTER HOOKS

I have read many a lament from writers who claim there is no reason for chapters in fiction. I can sympathize with the point of view since we don't want our readers to stop reading. Chapter breaks generally make convenient stopping points. I suggest we break that level of convenience.

To stop reading can break the flow and continuity of the story. It's death to the writer as readers may struggle to pick the story back up to continue.

Mystery writers are masters of the hook. Many of them use more barbs, snags, and hooks than opening day of trout season. Hence, the mystery part of their work. Their goal is to remove a who, what, where, when, why, or how in such a manner that the reader keeps at the story until that gap has been filled in. A good mystery writer may take out two, three, or even four of the basic story elements. The reader must search for clues along with the primary character to discover the missing pieces.

All genres, not just mysteries, require hooks. Otherwise, we might as well read the phone book. Adventure hooks are often an inkling of impending action or danger. Example: "Look out, Bob. The smugglers have a gun." Romance stories use emotional hooks to tug at a reader's heartstrings. Example: "How can Bob be so cruel? What? Bob is on the phone?"

Watch for opportunities to write hooks. Many locations will leap off the page as we write.

Keep the primary and secondary characters in trouble. Sure, they're nice people. We made them and our natural urge is to protect them. Avoid those natural urges. We should stay up late at night thinking of every dastardly thing we can throw at them. Our readers will crawl out of bed bleary-eyed in the morning because they just had to know how the character reacted or how they got out of that mess. Think old time movie serials. Think cliffhangers. Think of previews to coming attractions.

If we have written for a hundred pages and not added a hook, we are falling down on the job. We have probably just wasted 99.7 pages on a description of fall leaves in New England. Leave it out unless it moves the story. Poetic license is nice and adds a pretty touch, but if a reader wants to see Vermont foliage, they can look up a picture on the internet.

I call this section Chapter Hooks because the end of a chapter is exactly where we write a hook. Mark it as a chapter and move on. Near the beginning of the next chapter is where we tie the two chapters together.

WRITE THE CLIMAX FIRST
It is said that the hardest paragraph to write is the first paragraph of any book. So, don't start there.

Remember rule number three? We don't have to write a book in the same order we read the book.

Write the end first. Then back up and get the characters to the end as quickly as possible.

We became writers because we were readers first. Our natural inclination is to write our novel like we read a book, from front to back, beginning to end, start to finish. That just isn't always the correct or best way. We write in any order that gets us writing and keeps us writing. Sometimes we see the climax, the battle scene, the love scene, or the shootout more clearly in our imagination than other parts of our story. Write the parts we see clearly first if that's what it takes to get us started.

The biggest challenge most writers face is the blank page. That cold, clean, blank page is sitting there. It's empty and naked; daring us to make a mark, make an impression, to do something. That blank page stares us directly in the eyes and says, "*The Three Musketeers*, *Last of the Mohicans,* and *Bill the Galactic Hero* have already been written. What are you going to do to compare to those great works of literature?" Ignore the paper's taunts. The biggest, yet worst kept, secret in writing is that the blank page is a liar.

Eighth grade journalism teaches us to jam who, what, where, when, why and how into the first few paragraphs. We are not in journalism school. We are fiction writers. Fiction writers need to grab their reader's attention in the opening paragraph. It is not necessary to inform our readers of everything in the first paragraph.

I have said that getting started writing is difficult. I have repeated it because it *is* hard. Believe me when I say that chapters five through thirty-five will come a lot easier than the first paragraph. That is why we practice writing first paragraphs. We don't start with the first paragraph if we're stuck, unless we have a spare first paragraph handy.

Writing a book need not be like reading a book or watching a movie. It isn't always a simple point A to point B to point C and onward. There are no rules that say we can't write the major crisis first, and then backtrack, backfill and back up to get the characters to the crisis point of the story. We can write the battle scene first if we are writing military fiction. We can write the love scene first if we are writing a romance novel. We can write the big zombie attack, the big western shootout, the trial, the robbery or the devastating earthquake that flattens Sycamore Hills, North Dakota before we write character development.

BACK COVER BLURBS

The back cover blurb of every book contains a teaser designed to attract the potential reader. It tells them a bit about the who, the what and the troubles awaiting. Blurbs tease readers about the story, the issues, and possible resolutions to those tribulations. enticing a reader to pay hard-earned cash to find out the answers to the questions: what, why, who, how, or when.

Back cover blurbs do not have written resolutions. That is the purpose of the manuscript. We practice writing teasers, back covers, and blurbs to learn to entice readers and to get the imagination fired up.

WRITE THE BACK COVER BLURB EXERCISE

Write a back cover blurb. Write between 250 and 300 words. Don't write the resolution to this back cover blurb.

This back cover blurb exercise doesn't need to be the one you use for your first manuscript. Remember, this is an exercise. Write another back cover and then another. Write these until you are comfortable with putting down on paper the troubles your protagonist falls into.

Do not discard these back cover exercises. They may someday become your best seller.

SECTION THREE: KEEP WRITING

3.1 ONLY WE CAN DETERMINE WHAT HELPS OR HINDERS OUR WRITING EFFORTS

ENVIRONMENT

What surroundings do we choose to stimulate our creative juices? Writers must discover this for themselves. Environments can vary as wildly as the stories we tell. The goal is to develop a place that helps us write.

The urban myth states a famous writer wrote the series on youthful wizards while sitting in coffee shops. True or not, I would find people coming and going seriously distracting. Talking, laughing, the odor of food, and odd music would rapidly derail my train of thought. I have also read about a writer who put her desk and computer in her children's playroom. Gaak! Of course, she wrote children's books and a newspaper column about children.

Rule number one applies here; there are no rules. It isn't stupid if it works.

I have an office with a large empty desktop and a comfortable chair. I have a computer and monitor, properly devoid of games, email, Facebook and other distractions. I have a strong light and a window with open blinds. The window is behind me. This works for me. What works for you?

Trial and error, with a few exceptions, helps a writer determine their most productive environment. We may want to track our writing progress and related environmental factors to determine our optimum creative space. If I could write a thousand words an hour with a cat in my lap, then by any means I would go out and get a cat. Conversely, if the cat interrupted me enough that my progress fell off to only three hundred words an hour, then I would lock the cat out of the room, feed it to the dog, or sell it to the nearest Burmese restaurant.

We must have an environment we can control. A few environmental items are *must haves*. These factors may determine our success or failure. This isn't a writing issue. It's a control issue. We must be in control of our workspace and our tools.

Light
Proper lighting to do the job is required.

Air
Air shouldn't be a topic of much discussion. We all use it. We all need it. However, if it is too stuffy in our writing space we will fall asleep. If that's the case, we haven't been writing, we've been daydreaming.

Temperature
If our writing space is too warm, it'll make us sleepy. Hence, we must be King of the Thermostat. Temperature should be in the Goldilocks Zone. Just like her porridge, it shouldn't be too warm or too cold. Only the writer can determine the ideal temperature for their best work environment. I have read of a writer who takes his laptop and a chair into the field behind his house and accepts whatever weather God gives him.

Writing Medium

If a writer uses pen and paper to write, they must ensure they have plenty of paper and pens that work ... lots of pens. I use a computer; it comes with a lot of extra cyberbits already built in and is available for use.

Writing Space

Don't confuse it with the bill paying space, the letters to cousin Bob in the big, grey house space, or the junk mail opening space. We write where we write. That's what we're supposed to do when we sit there. If our writing space is too busy, we may find ourselves interrupted in the middle of our thoughts. Our thoughts drive our creative activity. Attempt to keep interruptions to those times when the house in on fire or the dog ate the cat.

I suggest a plan to write at the kitchen table and always sit in one particular chair while eating at the table, then change chairs only to write. We let people know we are writing when we sit in that specific chair. Sit anywhere else when we aren't writing. Sitting in our special writing chair is a signal to all of those non-writing types living in our homes that we are now in the throes of imaginative genius. Now isn't the time to have someone ask, what's the capital of Wyoming (Cheyenne). Now isn't the time to have someone ask, what's the value of PI (3.1415 ...) or (apple, cherry or peach, depending on spelling). Now isn't the time to have someone ask, what is an Einstein-Rosenberg Bridge (a wormhole ... sort of).

DISTRACTIONS

Only the writer can determine what distractions help or hinder. Ignore all advice in this area, including mine. Does a ringing telephone or doorbell, a blaring television or traffic noise hinder or help the writing process? If it helps, keep it. Throw it out if it doesn't enhance your efforts. This is a trial and error process.

Music can help or hinder our writing efforts; it's an individual preference. I find different styles of music suits different genres:

- Rock and Roll has much the same rhythm as science fiction.
- Adult contemporary works well when writing romance novels.
- Classical works well when I write historical fiction.

I know a few writers who must have complete silence. Even though there are no rules, we must determine if it helps, hinders, or in some bizarre way doesn't make any difference whatsoever. Background noise comes in many varieties: music, white noise, street noise, children playing or simply as quiet as possible. We must choose what we need to get our writing done.

I write in my home office. I have a radio. I turn it on only when I'm writing. That is a signal that I'm writing. It's the signal for my spouse not to bug me unless the house is on fire, zombies are at the back door or the naked jogger's club has decided to run by our house.

Does this work? Sometimes, but mostly—well, no. That's because she's a spouse and not a robot. That's because we all know we can't train our spouses. All we can do is lay down the ground rules and hope they don't beat us over the head with our own rules.

Examples of my ground rules:
1. I keep the window shades down in my home office.
2. I have the ceiling fan on so the air doesn't get stuffy.
3. I use an upright chair with nothing on my desk to distract me except the keyboard and the monitor.
4. I put music on the radio, but it's genre specific. I don't need to listen to the theme of Star Wars if I'm writing science fiction, but music helps me hear the heartbeat of my story. I play music to feel the rhythm of my words. I find a radio station without a lot of talk or I play appropriate music on the CD player.
5. I've been known to shut off the ringer on the phone if it's one of those days where all I'm receiving is robo-calls from politicians and people selling siding.
6. I refuse to answer the doorbell because girl scouts don't sell cookies door-to-door anymore and there is no other valid reason to answer the door unless I have already invited someone over.

I'm a bit of a grinder. Novels are very long, and long novels are very, very long. It's just a hell of a lot of man-hours. I tend to just go in there, and if it comes, it comes. A morning when I write not a single word doesn't worry me too much. If I come up against a brick wall, I'll just go and play snooker or something or sleep on it, and my subconscious will fix it for me. Usually, it's a journey without maps but a journey with a destination, so I know how it's going to begin and I know how it's going to end, but I don't know how I'm going to get from one to the other. That, really, is the struggle of the novel. (Martin Amis)

TOOLS

Invest in the best possible tools to achieve the best possible results.

Are you the happiest when writing with pen and paper? I have met a number of writers who use this medium. It forces them to slow down and think about what they are writing into their story. I have met more than one writer who just likes the sound of a number two pencil on paper.

Do you enjoy pounding out words on a manual typewriter? If so, find a good repair shop and a place to get supplies. Oh, and remember to learn to type.

I suggest a new writer use a computer with a good word processing program. Computer programs make wordsmithing easier. Computers save our work when properly setup to perform that function and make backups to a thumb or flash drive. They also help autocorrect our misspellings, but don't blindingly trust the spell checker or the grammar checkers. True editing is for later because our computer is a machine, not a rational thinking person. There are even voice programs that turn our speech into the written word.

I can see the lure of using a voice recorder. Simply tell the story and a voice recorder picks it all up. If this is your preference, you will eventually need to invest in a willing typist if you ever want your story read. A person whose story never finds its way onto paper or into digital format for readers is not a writer, but a storyteller. One way around this is to purchase and use speech recognition software. It will type out the story as you speak.

PHYSICAL EXERCISE

This isn't literary exercise, but physical activity. This involves getting the heart rate up and maybe even breathing a little harder than usual.

Writing is a butt expanding activity because the only way to write is to sit our butts in the chair and write. The form of exercise is between you and your doctor. Even a short brisk walk is worth its weight in gold. Yes, I know the more we exercise the less we weigh and walking itself has no mass, therefore no weight. The gold is literary gold. I have resolved many, many, many more literary conundrums by taking a long walk than I ever have by watching reruns on television or updating my Facebook page. I realize the phrase long walk is a relative term. The length of our walks is our choice.

We have many exercise choices. Select an activity designed to get the blood moving and the oxygen pumping to the brain yet doesn't use much brain power. Running, cycling, and swimming all come readily to mind. Yet, each has its drawbacks for our purposes.

I emphasis walking because it is an exercise that has proven to lower the risk of dementia, Alzheimer's, heart disease and Type 2 Diabetes. Unlike many cardiovascular exercises, it can be done (mostly) without much input from the brain. Our body moves while our brain is left to inhabit our imaginary world. This is the case because most of us have been doing this walking thing longer than anything else in our lives except eating and pooping.

Use walking time as a thinking activity. Keep something handy to jot down a note or two, to record that literary insight, or to call ourselves and leave a message about how to get Scooter out of the jam he is in. This literary light bulb may not go off the first time we walk. Keep at it.

Use this time to think about the story. Walking is great exercise, it can be done at surprisingly low cost and with a ready-made walking arena. This may not be the case if you live in International Falls, Minnesota or Bullhead City, Arizona. Walking in those places may be hampered by outdoor temperatures of below -20 or above 110 degrees. Invest in a treadmill if you live in such places, or if you don't like it outside. Remember, our purpose for walking is mental exercise; the physical benefits are the free extras. Keep the television off and don't prop a book or a magazine up on your treadmill while walking.

Physical activity fills the brain with oxygen and endorphins to fuel our imagination. Vacuuming and dusting are exercises that show rapid and positive results. We aren't exercising to shrink that ever expanding waistline; we're exercising to expand that ever shrinking brain.

Writing may be a physically challenging activity if you suffer from back pain. Any chronic pain diverts storyline flow. Do what you need to do to not hurt. Use pills, patches, and physicians, as necessary.

HYDRATION
Drink something while we write. The human body, our brains in particular, require fluid. Dehydration can cause lightheadedness and headaches, both of which can severely limit our imaginative output. We write something and drink something while we write: water, tea, lemonade, fruit drinks, and above all—a little more water.

SETTING GOALS AND REWARDS

We must teach ourselves to adhere to a system of goals and rewards. Structure a system of major and minor goals; the more difficult the goal the more valuable the reward. What goals can we set to keep us fighting past those dreaded blank pages?

- Chapter goals
- Word count goals
- Page count goals
- Writing until I kill someone goals (literary death only, please)

Rewards should be what motivates you, not what motivates me. More time to write is my primary motivation. What a wonderful self-fulfilling circle! What rewards can we offer for each goal?

- Special lunch with friends
- Hot fudge sundae
- Sex in the produce section at the grocery store
- An extra glass of wine at supper
- A week in Tahiti

Finishing our manuscript is a goal and a reward all on its own.

I love deadlines. I love the whooshing noise they make as they go by. (Douglas Adams)

SCHEDULE ACTIVE WRITING TIME

When we have time scheduled to write, if what we are writing does not work, then we write something else. Vacuuming, dusting, or having sex with our respective spouses may be fun, but it isn't writing. We don't do something else if what we're writing doesn't work.

This is the time we spend actually pounding the keys, dragging ink out of a pen, or speaking into a recording device. Pencils? Really? I think I have one around here somewhere, but they need sharpening too often and that interrupts the flow and rhythm of writing—that is the rhythm and flow of the activity and what is actually getting on paper.

How much time do you have? I average about a thousand words per hour. A 100,000 word novel is hundred hours or about two and a half weeks writing full time. A quick 60,000 word science fiction story is a little over a forty-hour work week from butt in the seat to slapping "The End" on the last page.

Writing part time. Most of us go to work, have family, commitments, and church may be a priority, so full time writing isn't realistic. Scheduling specific or flexible writing time may be required.

Give yourself time to read other people's work. It's an excellent opportunity to learn.

Time scheduling is a writing space control activity. Gaining the cooperation of spouses, significant others, and our children will work wonders for our productivity.

A creation of importance can only be produced when its author isolates himself; it is a child of solitude. (Johann Wolfgang von Goethe)

Scheduled writing time is set aside to do just that—write. Writers have two types of time available to them, writing time and non-writing time. Our writing time doesn't include going to buy new pens, getting coffee, walking the dog or defragging the computer. These tasks must be done on our non-writing time.

LENGTH OF TIME
How much time should we schedule for active writing? Our only guidelines are consistency and adherence. Try to schedule at least four days a week, never giving ourselves more than two days off in a row. This keeps us consistently writing and developing a writing habit. Do what we say we are going to do, adhere to our schedule. Prominently post this schedule so our spacemates remember and agree to help us meet our goals.

This isn't the time we spend daydreaming about our stories, the time we spend imagining our characters, or the time we spend doing research on whether there is or is not an oil refinery in Nacogdoches, Texas. I don't mean we can't stop and think. Thinking is good, just not to the point it interrupts our writing. Go for a walk if thinking is necessary. However, if we go for a walk we must remember to take a pencil and paper or a voice recorder. Do not take a laptop. They get too heavy after the first few hundred yards.

Get busy writing if the time is scheduled.

I am a galley slave to pen and ink. (Honore de Balzac)

SCHEDULING TIME BLOCKS

We do not need large blocks of time, just a consistent and realistic schedule. We should try for blocks of time large enough to energize our imaginations. Some fires burn fast and hot, some smolder and smoke for a while. We need to learn what kind of writer we are. We must give ourselves enough time to learn how effective we are in a given period.

If a writer can't skip watching nightly re-runs of *M*A*S*H*, they shouldn't schedule that time for writing.

Writing a book is a horrible, exhausting struggle, like a long bout of some painful illness. One would never undertake such a thing if one were not driven on by some demon whom one can neither resist nor understand. (George Orwell)

MAKE WRITING A HABIT

Deadlines

November is National Novel Writing Month (NaNoWriMo). Reportedly, more than a hundred thousand people attempt to start, write, and complete a novel in November. Many writers succeed. They make it so. We can, too!

Goals

We should write down our goals and place them where we can see them. Sample goals:

- word count
- page count
- finished chapter
- set the next hook
- I finally killed off that a-hole and now I can move on.

Celebrate successes.

Setbacks
Don't be afraid of failing to meet a goal. Fear holds a writer back. It's okay to set timelines, just know that they aren't life or death requirements. They are adjustable if necessary.

Publish your Schedule
This enables others around us to assist us by holding us to our schedule. Print it out and hang it on the office door. Give it space on your Facebook page. Post it on the fridge. It ain't real until it's on paper. Note: writing on a Facebook page may be fiction, but it isn't real writing.

Protect your Writing Schedule
Don't answer the phone. Don't go to the door. We may have to talk to our kids or spouse, but if they are over the age of eight—the children, not the spouse—they will understand when we tell them to not bother us when we are writing.

3.2 KEEP WRITING

WRITER'S BLOCK

Writer's block is the mental traffic jam that stops all forward progress. There are as many causes as there are writers, just as there are as many ways to overcome writer's block as there are people who have successfully overcome it. It's the snare of the blank page, an evil little beastie whose whole existence is ruined by a page full of story.

Writer's block is the imaginative mind becoming bored. If a writer is bored, the characters in the story will be boring, and the reader will be just as bored. Now is not the time to stop writing, but to throw something unexpected at the characters. Change their lives. Be nasty to them. Throw them under the bus, off the cliff, or let her see her boyfriend kissing her fourteen-year-old cousin. Mess with their lives enough and they won't be bored or boring. If our characters aren't bored, we won't be bored writing them.

KEEP WRITING

We can use a variety of methods over the course of a novel to prime the pump. There are multiple methods of writing stimulation. Some may be more effective than others. Before we know it, we are back to getting the story on paper.

Forcing the work will make it sound forced. Remember, deadlines are not life or death. The words will come; we cannot push them too hard. Here are some suggestions for us to consider:

1. Switch scene. If we're stumped and can't get started again, switch to writing a different scene in our story.

2. Put our primary novel aside for a few moments and write down a good storyline for your story file. By this point in our lives, we have more than one storyline in our heads. Remember this is just a short moment, as if we are taking a deep breath before a long sprint down the racetrack. Our primary story is still on the stove. It will burn and stick to the bottom of the pot if we don't get back to it soon.
   a. Use one of the practice exercises to get our literary muscles warmed up.
   b. Take the time to fill in some gaps in an existing story from our story file. This doesn't mean we begin writing our second novel at the same time.
3. Use a stop writing marker (SWM) in a variety of ways. The SWM clearly illustrates the location we stopped writing for the day. We want them to stand out so they are easy to spot when looking for them. Place them after the last line written. I use a long row of XXXXXs as my SWM. I know other writers who highlight a sentence or paragraph to make it stand out. It's your choice. How do we use the SWM?
   a. If you've hit a mental block, back up to your SWM and read what you've already written. This may jumpstart your creativity.
   b. Place your SWM and continue writing. Somewhere along the line you will sit down to write and BAM, nothing. Simply return to the SWM buried somewhere in the text. Remove it and pick up the narrative as you read. You don't change this nor amend that. Ignore grammar errors, you aren't editing yet. You aren't even stretching your literary muscles. You're simply warming up for a

running start. When you arrive at the end of the narrative, place a new SWM and just as quickly, continue on with the story, leaving this SWM in place for the next time you get hung up.

Note: We save the section after the SWM that we set aside. We don't throw it away just in case our second attempt sucks pond water and we need to go back to our first attempt. The goal was simply to get us writing again. Remember to save both versions using different names. For example, pondwater1A and pondwater1B.

    c. Rewrite it from memory. This method is a bit more drastic. Back up to the SWM and place all of the text you've written after that point aside. Now, write this text from memory. It may surprise aspiring novelists to find that their second attempt to cover the same ground results in a better literary effort than their first attempt. We must work to push our story beyond where we were stuck earlier.

    d. Change directions. Go back up to the SWM and place all of the text you've written after that point aside. Don't rewrite it from memory; instead take the story onto a different direction. This method is also a bit drastic. What is the next crisis or where is the next crossroads in the story? Take your story into a completely different direction than you initially headed.

4. Stop writing in the middle of a sentence when done writing for the day. This method is a preventative action. It may help give us a running start tomorrow.

It may also keep us awake all night with ideas on where to go with the story tomorrow.

In time, we may discover our own methods for breaking a stall, in the meantime, adapt one of mine. The main point is to have scheduled the time to write. We should honor the schedule and keep at it. Besides, continuing to write will anger the blank page resulting in our having beaten it for another day.

DO NOT EDIT
We do not edit as we go. Editing slows us down. It may throw up those mental roadblocks known as writer's block. We may end up spending more time trying to find a reliable source that tells us where that comma should or should not go than we spend writing our story. Let's get on with writing the story. Let it go and let the words flow. Actions we may take while writing our first draft:

- Ignore what we have written
- Write awhile with your eyes closed
- Write awhile with the monitor off
- Shut off spell check and grammar check for the first draft
- Write, even if it doesn't make sense

Write fast, edit slow. Writing and editing are two separate steps. There may come a time when we can do both at once, but not now. Many people have learned to dance without looking at their feet, but it takes practice.

RECORD OUR THOUGHTS

We should always have a way to record our thoughts when we aren't writing. Trust me; we won't remember the good ideas by the time we get home.

A voice recorder may work well, but saying "Remember to kill Bob on Tuesday" may get a person more than funny looks on a crowded elevator.

Pen and paper are generally good. I say generally because many of us have to stop what we're doing and jot down those elusive thoughts. Then there is the dreaded, "Honey, where did I put my notebook?".

Using a Smart Phone / tablet / iPad for notes can work. How fast can you type with your thumbs? I am a bit of a Luddite. Technology can be wonderful. I do my writing on a computer, but technology brings its own level of challenges. "Honey, where did that file go?"

One caveat. Do NOT write while driving. Our book may be the next *Gone With the Wind*, but it's not worth our lives. Pull over and jot it down when we have a truly stunning revelation.

RECORD OUR OBSERVATIONS

Writers should learn to listen more and not just hear. We should focus on listening to the conversations around us, not just hear the buzz of words. Listen to the way other people talk and write down the strange, unusual, or just amusing conversations around us. Three examples of actual conversations I overheard:

Three women on an elevator; woman A to woman B: "Your car accident was so bad that I worry every time I get in my car."
Woman B to the woman A: "I pray every time I get in the car now."
Woman C to the woman B: "Everyone prays when you get behind the wheel."

Woman on a crowded elevator in a three-story building: "Anybody going higher than three today?"
Woman in the back of the crowd: "Not unless you know something about this elevator that I don't."

Woman to a man at a lunch table: "Am I crazy or did it get cloudy outside?"
Man's response: "What makes you think that is an either / or question?"

Most people do not listen with the intent to understand; they listen with the intent to reply. (Stephen R. Covey)

Many people only listen with half an ear to a conversation. Instead of focusing on what is being said, they are thinking about what they are going to say or the joke they want to tell. Learn to sit back and actively listen, even to those conversations we have not been invited to join. It all becomes fodder for our writing.

You get the idea here: writers strive to be active observers not passive listeners. Learn to see the forest AND the trees. Can we describe what we observe? Can we explain why they call that Arizona canyon Grand or why they use the word giant to describe the redwoods in California? Are we observing the people in the department store or are they just obstacles in our way? Can we describe the taste of blue or the feel of salty?

Every reader finds himself. The writer's work is merely a kind of optical instrument that makes it possible for the reader to discern what, without this book, he would never have seen in himself. (Marcel Proust)

We have five senses: sight, hearing, touch, taste, and smell. Our job as writers is to observe the world around us, using our words to paint pictures in our reader's minds using all five senses.

STAY AWAY FROM THE INTERNET

We shouldn't have to discuss this, but it's a time waster. It may be a wonderful research tool, but we aren't doing research, we're writing. Don't use the internet when you are on fire, writing ninety-to-nothing and you just need to know the name of the indigenous pine trees growing on the coast of Washington State. We only think we need to know. We don't have to write —Jill stood in the forest of yellow and loblolly pines. We should write—Jill stood in the pine tree forest. We can fill in the rest later—if it becomes necessary to the flow of the story, otherwise who cares? Get on with the story.

WRITER'S BLOCK EXERCISES

1. Reading other writer's works

Read something someone else wrote that we've already read, especially if it is something we do not want to read again. We compliment the reading by making notes on what changes we would have made and how we would write it differently. Are we getting words on paper? Good! Now is the time to get back to our story.

2. Read the Yellow Pages

This should become boring faster than watching C-Span reruns. In a flash, our minds will begin to wander and daydream. The second we recognize we're daydreaming, get back to writing the story.

3. Time capsule

We've been asked to prepare a time capsule filled with items that will tell future generations what life was like in our own time. What will we include? Make a list of the items.

4. Flexing the dictionary

Pick three random words from the dictionary. Write something with these three words in it.

5. It's the news

Newspapers and magazines provide great ideas. Pick an article from a newspaper or magazine and use it to inspire a story or poem. We could also write a letter to the editor in response to the article.

6. What does the picture say

Pick an old photograph or picture in a magazine. Study it for a few moments and write something about it.
- Who is in the picture?
- How old are they?
- Where are the headed?
- What has just happened to them?
- Why are they in the picture?
- What else can we see in the picture that may be important?
- What about a title?

7. Proverbs and quotations

Pick a proverb or quotation. Ensure we understand its meaning and use it to write a story, essay, or blog.

8. Adding silly stuff

One other possibility that I have heard of—although I've never tried it myself—is to insert something completely ludicrous into our story. Have aliens enter the room and start killing everybody with death rays in a cozy mystery. Have our character do the exact opposite of what she's been telling everybody she has planned on doing. We won't be using this material, but it might free up our imaginations. Who knows, we could come up with something we can use someday.

9. Classified ads

So, we're stuck again and need something to hammer away at the writer's block, the dreaded blank page's most effective weapon. This exercise *doesn't* take place in our story and it will most likely never grace the pages of our manuscript. The design of this exercise is to get us thinking about the people, places, and times of our story. There are two ways to do this.

1. For the hero of our story, write a classified advertisement for a newspaper, e-zine, or the town crier, that he might read or hear in a quiet moment with a cup of coffee, a cold beer, or a cheap cigar by his campfire. We should be as precise as we can in our description of his surroundings. For example:

   - early morning with his feet up on the horse rail in front of the general store just about sunrise
   - late at night in the Hollywood diner with only a fat waitress and a skinny cook to keep him company
   - Ten Forward on a slow night in deep space

   What type of ad would catch our hero's attention? Is it a good buy? Does he really need another one? Or is this just like the car that the dead guy was driving that night?

2. For the heroine of our story, write a classified advertisement for a newspaper, e-zine, or the office bulletin board at the church that she might write if she had something to offer for sale. Be as precise as we can about people, places, and chronology as she writes the advertisement and thinks about what she is selling and why she wants to get rid of it.

   - What genre and time period specific items would she have that she wants to sell?
   - Why is she selling?
   - Does she really need the money?

- Why is she putting it in this type of format and not selling it on-line?
- What type of people is she trying to entice into calling her about this advertisement?

10. Finishing incomplete sentences

Take a sentence from anywhere. Be careful not to read the whole sentence. Use the newspaper, a familiar book, or a magazine. Write down the first five words of the sentence and then finish the sentence yourself. Write it again and finish it again. Write it as if our protagonist would finish it.

Once we realize we're thinking about and writing about our story, get back to it.

3.3 FIND OR START A WRITERS' GROUP CONSISTENT WITH OUR GENRE AND STYLE

OPEN WRITERS' GROUPS

An open group is one where anyone can walk through the door and sit down. They advertise on-line, in the local papers, and on the bulletin board at the grocery store. Becoming a member is simply signing up and showing up as there isn't any vetting process.

An open writers' group typically meets at the local library or a school. There are forty-eleven writers who show up to hear a speaker talk about the Dewey Decimal System, then they eat cookies and maybe discuss someone's writing. There may be a few writers in the group with skill and the ability to share their skill, but they may be hard to find and even harder to get into their already overcrowded breakout discussion groups.

Most open writers' groups are not designed for writers working on a first draft. Listening about other people's writing issues is not making the best use of our time. Why are we talking about writing to strangers, when we should be writing? The time for attending these groups is after we have completed our first draft and have something to contribute to the discussion. This doesn't mean we shouldn't interact with other writers and attend writing seminars or lectures by published authors. Attend and participate in as many of these as possible. Just be wary of groups who take up your time with little to no return.

Large writers' groups may offer breakout sessions, but may not break down into genre specific sub-groupings. Generally, these groups are comprised of people writing in a variety of genres. A children's book author may not be the best sounding board for discussing a medical suspense story about a flesh-eating virus. There are some lonely people pretending to be aspiring writers who'll waste our time talking about something they're going to write. We can usually recognize these people as the ones who bring cookies to the meeting instead of their manuscript.

There are a few good, and many not so good writers' groups on the internet. We should be wary of who we're talking to. It's not that they will steal ideas, but we may have more skill and experience than they do. They might be in that ninety-eight percent of would-be writers who cannot even finish their first draft. Their advice may not be based on sound literary theory or practical application.

Listen carefully to first criticisms made of your work. Note just what it is about your work that critics don't like—then cultivate it. That's the only part of your work that's individual and worth keeping. (Jean Cocteau)

CLOSED OR PRIVATE WRITERS' GROUPS

These groups are comprised of only invited authors and are for members only. They are formed around specific genres such as the Romance Writers of America or the Science Fiction and Fantasy Writers of America. Attendance at one meeting may be offered for prospective members or it may be by invitation only.

Do you require story progress feedback? Most writers do. They find other readers and writers in the same genre and bounce ideas back and forth. Writing isn't the complete isolation activity that it sounds like. I recommend finding or starting a group consistent with our chosen genre and style.

If you show someone something you've written, you give them a sharpened stake, lie down in your coffin, and say, 'When you're ready'. (David Mitchell)

Many stories are improved by comments, such as: "Did you think about this? What about that? That isn't how a football reacts when thrown in zero gravity without standard rotational pull." Or even, "Sorry dude, but you had the guy saluting with his right hand, but that hand was blown off three chapters earlier." These casual comments are the results of showing what you've already written to a group of authors and readers. Most such input only requires an acknowledgement by the author, usually in the afterword. It isn't plagiarism or fraud to incorporate those ideas. Most people are pleased to be involved in our writing process.

3.4 OUR FIRST GOAL IS TO GET OUR STORY WRITTEN

A book is the only place in which you can examine a fragile thought without breaking it, or explore an explosive idea without fear it will go off in your face. It is one of the few havens remaining where a man's mind can get both provocation and privacy. (Edward P. Morgan)

POINTS OF VIEW

Point of View (POV) is who is telling the story. It defines the narration style, determines the way a reader hears the tone and sets the angle of the unfolding story. The POV is key in the reader's understanding of the narrative. It can offer or withhold access to backstory, history and some character's thoughts, desires and insights. Any POV, including multiple points of view, will work in fiction.

First Person
First Person POV is where a character narrates the story, acting as their own storyteller. "I ran to my car." This is a difficult point of view as it limits what we can and cannot know. We can only know what we do, what we hear, and what we see. We cannot know what Bob is thinking or what Betty has done, unless we watch Betty do it or Bob speaks up and tells us what he is thinking. Primary pronouns used are: me, my, I, mine.

Second Person
Second Person is the rarest used POV. It makes the reader the protagonist in the story. "You ran to your car." This is included here as a matter of completeness. I have been told this point of view works well with children's stories. Sorry, I just don't get it. Maybe you are a better writer than I am

and can make it work. Primary pronouns used are: you, your.

Third Person
Third Person POV is where we write another person's story as an outsider looking in on the action. "John ran to his car." This is certainly the most common POV and can be the most successful narrative style. It's the most popular in fiction and the easiest to write. Primary pronouns used are: he / she, they, their.

For success, we must define our third person profile before we begin to write. We must, repeat must, continue with this profile throughout our manuscript or story. A third person POV profile is simply how much we can know of our protagonist's thoughts, feelings, desires and unspoken plans.

- Objective Profile. The narrator—you—doesn't have access to the primary character's feelings, thoughts or motivations. The primary character has closed his mind to us. "John ran to his car."

- Subjective Profile. The narrator—you again—has access to what the primary character feels, thinks, hopes, wishes and daydreams about. The protagonist is an open book to us. "In his excitement over the coming date with Irene, John ran to his car, daydreaming of kissing her."

These third person profiles are on a sliding scale from limited knowledge all the way up to omniscient and god-like where we can know everything that goes on in the heart of our protagonist.

Please be aware that if we define a subjective point of view for our primary character, we should not grant ourselves subjective omniscient capabilities for our secondary and tertiary characters. Oh, we can do this, but it is very risky and we will lose our third person point of view credentials. In third person, if we want our readers to know the heart and mind of our protagonist's lover, then we should have the lover tell our lead character what they are thinking. Our secondary characters can talk, can't they? Besides, this is fiction, not real life where the lover won't say a thing except "what's on TV tonight?"

Alternating Person
Alternating POV is difficult for a first time writer. I suggest avoiding altering the storyline person point of view on our first novel. We should focus on writing for our main character. Focus on what happens to him or her. An alternate perspective in the narrative will certainly explain the motivations of our secondary characters concerning their relationship and reactions to the primary character. It can make a well-rounded story reach other perspectives in the narrative. But, it can be difficult for new writers to maintain a clear and precise storyline path using alternating person POV.

Liar's Point of View
Liar's POV can be great fun. This perspective is where we leave the reader in doubt as to the trustworthiness of our narrator. This can be a very difficult point of view and I don't recommend it for your first novel. I only include it here for the sake of completeness. Or maybe not; recently I was told I was already an accomplished liar before I started writing.

OUTLINING THE STORY

We base our outlines on one-sentence turning points and scenes. Delete any scene from our outline that doesn't move the story. That doesn't mean we pare our work down to simple action or activity. We should consider our outline as a series of railroad ties used only as support for the rails. This outline is a base foundation. Flowery and descriptive language is what will flesh out our work. Expand the outline by adding dialogue and conflict. Delete any scene from our outline that does not contain dialogue or conflict, thereby, moving the story.

Deletions
Deletions are painful, but sometimes necessary. Amputation can stop the spread of gangrene and the odor of rotten cheese. Do not be afraid to throw the whole outline away. We may find that halfway through our work, our characters are beginning to rebel against the actions we have planned for them. Why? Because they have developed personalities and motivations that deny these actions. Scrap the outline or change it to fit what the characters would do.

TIMELINES

Define the timeline. This need not be specific. It's necessary to keep our storyline within the realm of believability. Don't worry about dates, but we need to know how much time the story takes:

- One day long = keep track of the hours
- One week long = keep track of the days
- Years long = keep a detailed calendar

Be accurate on timeliness. Don't we all hate those cowboy movies where they send a horseback rider from Wyoming to Kansas and the buckaroo is back in two days? Even the best horse cannot get from Jackson Hole to Dodge City and back again that fast. Fifty miles per day on a horse is the rule of thumb, but only if the cowpuncher has a tough butt and a good horse.

Keep your timeline handy. You'll be surprised at how often you'll need to refer to it.

AVOID FLASHBACKS

Try to avoid flashbacks, use them sparingly if absolutely necessary. Not only is this very difficult to write from a grammar perspective, but it's hell-on-wheels damaging to story rhythm. That doesn't mean we can't use this literary tool on our third, sixth or thirty-sixth book. It's just my suggestion to avoid its use for our first novel.

Tell the story from front to back. Put the flashback in the story in chronological order if the information is necessary to the story. For the first novel, keep the timeline straight from beginning to end. Most writers will find it much easier to write and our readers will find it much easier to read. Give the backstory to the reader in little bits throughout your novel. It adds suspense to your storyline keeping the reader wondering how things got this bad in the first place. Tickle your reader with tidbits, dropping morsels as they read. Write the sequence in chronological order only if the backstory is necessary to understand how the characters reached this point in their lives.

AVOID DATA DUMPS

Many writers tend to start off their work with a few exciting pages, then in some magical way, the writer is overcome with literary diarrhea. The reader must then wade through pages and pages of backstory. The author's intention is to give the reader information necessary to understand the story set up. This has been described to me as a literary data dump.

I recently read a novel that was very well written except for the thirty pages of backstory between pages three and thirty-three. It almost persuaded me to put the book away. My suggestion to the author—yes, I emailed her—was to take the backstory out and leave it up to the reader's imagination. Trust me, our readers have awesome imaginations. My second suggestion—and the best—was to turn the backstory into books one and two, leaving the existing novel as book three. Yes, there was enough of a storyline buried in those pages for two additional novels.

Avoid the technical data dump. Explaining how a combustion engine works isn't necessary when telling the reader that John started the car. Some explanation of technical specifications may be necessary depending on the type of fiction being written, but we shouldn't dump it on our reader in exposition. Have our characters discuss it, giving our reader the necessary information within the conversation. We shouldn't write our story assuming our reader knows so little that we must explain why cotton shirts are wrinkled coming out of the dryer.

LEAVE THE PUNCH LINE FOR THE END
Do not give the storyline twist away too soon. Remember, this is fiction. Our readers don't know what's going to happen. We aren't writing nonfiction where everyone already knows the Titanic goes down or that Amelia Earhart's plane goes missing. If our narrator is dead and telling us the story from the grave, keep that a secret until the end. Let our readers wonder whether the character lives or dies. Don't have our romantically challenged couple tell us the story of how they met and married as a flashback during their fiftieth wedding anniversary party. Let the reader be surprised as to whether they get together or not.

There is no real ending. It's just the place where you stop the story. (Frank Herbert)

3.5 A PERFECT TITLE

Titles are marketing tools. The title is a carefully crafted promise as to what the reader can expect. In fiction, this is a promise of entertainment and a good read. It's a big part of any book's first impression on a reader.

Consider the title temporary if the plan is to publish our book through a traditional publishing house. A writer can title their work anything they want to when they self-publish or publish through a print-on-demand company.

Book titles generally can't be copyrighted, but we want ours to stand out, to catch the eye of a potential reader. Search Amazon.com's book section to make sure a title hasn't been used. Check your specific genre and any closely related genre. Our book title should be unique.

Subtitles
Not only no, but h.e.double-hockey-sticks no. Not with fiction. Okay ... well, maybe if we plan on writing a series.

Genre Specific
Fit the title to our specific genre. Titles should reflect the content written or planned. It should fit within the general scope of the chosen genre. Scan through Amazon.com's book section for a list of existing titles. It should give us an idea of what a good title might be. Look for a consistent or recent pattern in top selling titles within our specifically chosen genre for this book.

Young adult and children's books often have titles composed of the lead character and the main theme, such as *Tiny Tim and the Christmas Turkey* or *Moses and the Water Gap*. Do not title a book "Burning Bodies" if the plan is to write a funny novel, unless the work is so funny it can overcome such a bad title. Do not title a book "Burning Bodies" if the plan is to write a romance novel. The writer may be thinking about bodies burning with desire, but to the potential reader it sounds like the subject is a serial killer.

Title Design
Pull words from the story's theme, plotline, outline, or basic story idea. Make a list of these words. Make heavy use of the thesaurus. Mix and match until one grabs our ears. List as many titles as we can imagine and then choose one.

Short and Sweet
The shorter our title is, the better it will be. Can we shorten it to one word or two? For fiction, try not to go longer than five words, including the article(s) - a, an, and, the. Most full-length novels have the title, author's name, and publisher on the spine, so all this needs to be legible when the book sits on the bookshelf.

Syllable Cadence
We can work on syllable cadences if we keep a title short. The title of the published science fiction book, *Metal Boxes*, has four syllables with a heavy two-beat cadence, with the emphasis on the first syllable of both words.

Leading Character or Location
We can title our books after the lead character or a location in our book. *Larry Goes to Space* is the title of one of my recent manuscripts.

Rhyming Words
Depending on the genre, rhyming words make very catchy titles. *Jack's Back, Jill's Ill Will,* or even the long time classic, *Humpty Dumpty*.

Eye Catching Words
Contradictory words can catch the reader's eye. It makes the potential book buyer stop, look, and say "Whaaaat?" Here are some examples of using the five senses to spice up a title:

- The Salty Sky
- The Green Smell
- The Bright Touch
- The Loud Pudding
- The Smelly Red

Brainstorming
Work with your critique group or brainstorm team on title design. It's much more fun discussing a first novel named *The Ice of Wry* than it is to call it my book or project number one. I love some of my book titles, though my wife and I usually refer to them as number five or number eight when we're home alone.

Eye on The Prize is my first published literary work. This is a both a good and a bad title. I should'a, could'a, would'a selected a better title before publication.

- The bad: at the time I titled this book, no one had ever suggested checking Amazon's book section for novels with the same name. There are about a gazillion other books with the same title. None are in the same genre, but there are enough uses of the title that I should've gone with another title—had I looked.
- The good: The phrase "eye on the prize" comes from Philippians in the Bible and rings familiar in many reader's ears. In my book, it is a clever word play, as the prize refers to the name of a ship, a category of

ships taken in warfare, and the rewards for success. It gave me a consistent focus in writing the story.

An overused title only adds our book to the rest of the books in the forest of similar titles.

Steel Walls and Dirt Drops is my second novel. This title came about because of specific storylines in my head. It had the added benefit of sounding contradictory. Steel and dirt do not go together, so it catches the eye.

Chewing Rocks is my third novel. This is one of my favorite titles. What else would you call a science fiction book about asteroid mining?

Metal Boxes is my fourth book. This started out as a generic working title just shoved onto the title page of my work to hold the space until a valid title came along. As I wrote, I was able to add more parts to the story to fit the title. The title drove the character's flaws, actions, and reactions.

Chasing Harpo is my fifth book. The title is simple, but complementary in tone. A chase implies action and the name Harpo implies humor—or it does if you are a Marx Brothers fan.

Titanium Texicans is book six. Some among my brainstorming clan love this title and others hate it with a passion. Me? I am so non-committal that the first beta reader or editor who has a better idea will win a prize.

Larry Goes to Space is my seventh manuscript. Um— maybe not much of a title. We'll just have to see what Larry thinks about it.

The Friendship Stones, *The Granite Heart* and *The Heaviest Rock* form a trilogy. These titles were specifically written to be in alphabetical order by title when placed on the shelf: F-G-H. The first of the series was originally titled *The Friendship Rocks*, until it was pointed out that rocks has a different meaning in today's vernacular. So, I considered pebbles, gravel and stones to keep all of the titles in a rock category.

The Planet with No Name is my tenth manuscript. It's both a western and science fiction. As the name implies it combines elements of both genres. It's a play on words from a western movie from the sixties, *A Man with no Name*. Adding "the planet" moves it into the science fiction genre.

Driving Storyline
Titles can drive the storyline. Titles are important to our story. They can often add inspiration to a writer as they build the story around the title.

Keep the Title in Perspective
We do not delay our writing just to come up with a perfect title. Remember, we are not married to our title, we are not engaged to it, as a matter of fact, we are not even casually dating this title. It is, like our first novel, a work in progress. It may grow on us in later use or be discarded with disgust by the first editorial critique we are forced to endure.

3.6 AUTHOR'S NAME

Perform a search of your name. Do you remember I suggested doing a title search on Amazon.com? Perform an Amazon.com search on your name also. We may want to consider using a pen name. For example, Samuel Clemens wrote as Mark Twain. We may want to go by John Karl Rowling rather than using the name J.K. Rowling.

There are over one million books published every year. It is difficult enough for readers to find our books without them having to wade through pages of authors using the name S. King.

Suggestion—do not use initials. Initials increase internet search difficulty. Most search engines—and people who use them—become confused trying to figure out if the author used periods or spaces. It is hard enough for my readers to find me without trying to figure out if I am A Black, A. Black, AL Black, A.L. Black, A L Black, or even ALBlack. This can be fixed in the Search Engine Optimization and MetaData, but it's easier at this point to skip the whole initials problem by simply not using them.

SECTION FOUR: TYING IT ALL TOGETHER

4.1 ARE WE FINISHED?

PROLOGUES

Do not, not, not, not use a prologue. Many writers think of a prologue as a giant hook for their stories. It's not a hook. It's a story distraction. It's the orchestra warming up in the pit, having no bearing on the music to follow. Place anything the reader must know into the story. It'll easily fit if it's important. If it doesn't fit, the reader doesn't need to know. This bears repeating: our first and most important hook must be set within the first five paragraphs. Why isn't our prologue in chapter one if it is necessary to the flow of the story? That is a better location for story flow and readability.

Remember rule number four—the story takes as long as it takes.

CHAPTERS

Chapters are necessary in non-fiction, reference and research materials. They can be deadly to a fiction writer's first book. Try very hard to not make a big deal of them. Are chapters required? Absolutely not.

Remember, there are no rules to writing fiction. However, in fiction, chapters provide our readers with a sense of accomplishment and rhythm. They help readers gauge their progress through the story, like pauses in music give a singer an opportunity to draw a breath. Chapters also give us, the writer, something to celebrate and to measure our writing progress.

The good, the bad, the ugly of chapters. Chapters have their place in fiction as does punctuation, spelling, and grammar. Punctuation, spelling, and grammar are the people we borrowed money from; they are to be avoided whenever possible.

The Bible is a good example of why we use chapters. The oldest copies of the Bible were written in uncil format. Which of the following is easier to read:

- UNCILMEANSITISALLINCAPSWITHOUTSPAC
  ESANDWITHOUTPUNCTUATIONRUNNINGTH
  ROUGHTHEWHOLEBOOK
- Uncil means it is all in caps without spaces and without punctuation running through the whole book.

Length
What is the appropriate length for a chapter? Who cares. There are no rules. We put 'em where we want 'em.

Headings
It may be necessary in certain genres to add a title to each chapter. For example, if we're writing a book for young readers, "Bob and Jenny go to the market" or "Jim and Nancy help with the cleaning" are simple enough. I wouldn't suggest, "Klatharson Slays the Great Horned Dragon", unless it's an exceptionally strange children's book. Keep the text of the heading consistent with the intended reading level of the reader.

Chapter headings are something best left to our rewrite. Just slap a number on it for now and move on.

Hang it on a Hook

When we manage to slam-dunk a good story hook, we can use it as an excuse to put in a chapter break. When writing the rough draft of our first story, chapter hooks are the friends we yearn to spend time with.

Chapters will also help give us something to celebrate and to measure our writing progress.

QUOTES

Quotes between chapters serve as stepping-stones across the flow of the story. They are like rocks in the stream, causing the water to babble, but not saying anything. The best rocks don't interrupt the flow of the stream. They simply add a counter-point to the rhythm of the water. They should be added later if we want to use them. I recommend avoiding this literary device until later in a long writing career.

WORD COUNT

The first and foremost reason for an author to check word count is monitoring the day-to-day progress. It doesn't tell us when we are done writing for the day, nor does it indicate when our story is done. Counting the words has use within our scope of writing, it provides a benchmark for tracking our writing. It can form a sense of accomplishment that keeps us motivated.

Checking our word count gives us a rule of thumb on how our story is progressing. We may be too wordy if we have written ten thousand words and we still do not have our story out of the starting blocks. Remember, our story should flow. It's a stream, not a stagnant pond. We do know what becomes of stagnant ponds, right? They get scummy and stinky.

Word count gives us a sense of goal accomplishment. Where should we be in a word count when we're finished? Only our story can tell us. Writers gauge a story by when the story is complete and has been told from front to end, not by word count.

Place a running total of the word count at the top of every work. Put it on the first page above the title. That makes it easy for us to keep track of and easy to update as our work progresses.

Word count caution. We shouldn't pad our word count. A word count of 100,000 words may simply mean that we are too loose with our literary toolbox. Can we cut it back? Can we hack and chop at it to make it smaller, but still keep the same essence? And I do mean essence, because what is written must be, in our mind, essential not only to the story, but the flavor, the spice, and the intensity of the work.

I once had an agent tell me to pare a 140,000 word novel back to 80,000 words. She said this sight unseen, without so much as a look at the first five paragraphs. I told her that I would rather get another agent. We should have no problems with cutting words, but the paring must make sense, not just fit someone else's arbitrary number.

We all know agents want to make money, publishers want to make money, bookstores—what remain of them—want to make money. They want books with lower word counts because larger books demand higher prices and do not sell as rapidly as shorter, cheaper books.

We shouldn't take up writing if making money is our prime motivation. If that is the case, we should go into banking or buy a printing press.

Counting Words

A rule of thumb for typewritten pages is two hundred and fifty words per page. Word counts may be difficult to determine if a manuscript is written with pen and ink. Handwritten word counts may be much less than a typed work, depending on penmanship. Keep a three-ring binder for the written work.

It may be necessary to manually count. This becomes a matter of counting the words on a page. Then, try counting the number of pages written. This will vary between writers depending on how big and fancy their penmanship and what tools are used, ballpoint pen versus fountain pen. After that, it is simple third grade math: multiply number of words by page count.

Most modern word processors have an automatic word count function. The writer may have to learn where the command function is to find out their word count, but it beats performing a manual count.

Word Count Lengths

Publishers and agents gauge book lengths by word count. Rule of thumb word count lengths are included here to give us a sense of where we might be going with our first novel:

- Short story - less than 7,500 words
- Novelette - 7,500 to 18,000 words
- Novella - 18,000 to 40,000 words
- Novel - between 40,000 and 150,000 words
- Epic - more than 150,000 words
- Beyond 180,000 words - you may have a book and its sequel. It may be time to split them. That's your call. I'm just making the suggestion.

Guinness World Records 2012 lists the longest single book at 1,200,000 words. It is *In Search of Lost Time* by Marcel Proust. It's 4,211 pages long printed in seven volumes. To put this into perspective, consider the Harry Potter series by J.K. Rowling. It's 1,084,170 words published as a seven book series.

Remember, the rule of thumb says we can ignore the rule unless we are passionate enough about that rule to lose our thumbs.

Word Count Variations
In the literary world, word count can vary tremendously by genre. Please bear in mind that this will probably be out of date by the time you read this. Not only do publishers change their minds as often as junior needs his diapers changed, but e-readers will make genre word counts as old fashioned as horse and buggy rides. We still have horses and buggies these days, some people just like them, but the rest of us get around in cars. Current genre lengths:
- Commercial fiction - 60,000 to 100,000 words
- Mystery - 60,000 – 80,000 words
- Romance - 50,000 to 80,000 words
- Science Fiction and Fantasy - 80,000 to 100,000 words—However, the Science Fiction and Fantasy Writers of America organization states a Nebula Award must be a minimum 40,000-word novel. There are many published science fiction books longer than 150,000 words.
- Suspense - 80,000 - 100,000 words
- Westerns - 80,000 - 100,000 words
- Young Adult - 15,000 - 40,000 words

This isn't a complete list by any means. It is just a random sampling to give us an idea of where the publishing industry is going. We, as writers, should all be concerned about the journey, not the end result.

Some writers will fall short and attempt to pad their stories with unnecessary verbiage to make it fit some arbitrary standard in the publishing world. Avoid this temptation. Readers can tell if a story has been padded. That doesn't mean our story doesn't need a little bit of fleshing out. A little muscle wrapped around the bone makes our stories more appealing to our readers.

Watching the pages pile up can be as satisfying, or maybe more so, than watching the word count increase. It's our work and in the end, our happiness should prevail. After all of this, I recommend ignoring the rules as the story takes as long as it takes.

JOURNALING

Maintaining a log, writing diary or a journal helps us monitor our progress. We should list the essentials of each writing session:

- Start time
- Title of work
- Progression or word count
- Frustrations in our story telling
- Interruptions. For example: did the phone ring too often or did we have to drive the neighbor's cat to the veterinarian?
- End time

Specifically annotate items we should watch out for in our next writing session, such as:

- Creative thoughts we didn't have time to get to today
- Story twists
- Character changes
- Story inconsistencies that need changing

4.2 WHERE TO STOP

DON'T CHEAT OUR READER OUT OF A GOOD ENDING

In the end, we cannot use a character, location, machine, device, activity, piece of bread or a dirty hammer that we haven't previously introduced somewhere in our story. There are no magical believable endings.

Surprise endings are one thing, but having a zombie eat the hero will not endear us to our readers if the story didn't have zombies in it to begin with.

We may envision writing a trilogy or a series of sixteen novels, but each work must have a beginning, a middle, and for this purpose, an end. For our first novel, ensure the story reads as a standalone novel. This is good advice for that seventh novel, too. Our readers will thank us for it.

Readers deserve closure. I often tell my critics that nothing in life is ever wrapped up with a neat little bow; there are always things left undone. Many responses are similar to: "I'd go to work if I wanted real life. I read to get away from things left undone." It may be necessary to leave some small tidbit unfinished. We want our fans to read our next book and we don't want them so frustrated with unfinished business that they avoid our books altogether.

Always…and I mean always leave them wanting more. (Emma Nichols)

We've got to give our readers the opportunity to say goodbye to the characters.

We build our story as our protagonist struggles towards reaching his goal. Achieving or failing to achieve our main character's stated goal is our main climax. It's just a matter of tying up loose ends after that.

STORY THEFT
I have never seen it, but it is possible. This isn't an issue among professionals, we already have vast files of story ideas of our own and half-told tales rattling around the back corners of our minds. However, some writers' groups are filled with amateurs, many of whom have never finished, nor will they ever finish, their first draft. Bottom line here, don't even think about doing this.

COPYRIGHT
I said earlier that a title cannot be covered by copyright, neither can an idea. Anything written is already covered by U.S. Copyright. However, it is important to protect our work by registering the copyright. This can be done at http://www.copyright.gov. At the time of this publication it only costs $35.00 for registration and the site has a simple step-by-step process to follow.

How paranoid are or should we be about having our work stolen? Remember, this is our first novel. It may be the next *Of Mice and Men*, but probably not. A lawyer specializing in intellectual rights once told me to copyright anything I wrote before I show it to anyone, everything from the original outline to the last edited copy. This would involve multiple copyrights on the same story. I suggest we copyright our work before we share it with anyone we do not know and trust.

I recommend purchasing the book *Protecting Your Writings, A Legal Guide for Authors* by Maria Crimi Speth, ISB #978-1450243643. She is an intellectual property rights lawyer and her book covers a lot of protections and details for new authors to consider prior to publication.

Of all the diversions of life, there is none so proper to full up its empty spaces as the reading of useful and entertaining authors. (Joseph Addison)

SECTION FIVE: WRAPPING IT UP

5.1 FINAL POINTS

GRAMMAR AND EDITING
Ignore them both for now. We couldn't care less about editing and grammar in our first draft. Ignore grammar. Ignore punctuation. Ignore spelling. Ignore formatting.

Write, don't edit. Try not to edit any writing on the first draft. Our first draft is all about our story. It's our plot. It isn't chiseled in stone. I only mention it here because we should use enough grammar correctly when we write that when we sit down to do our first rewrite we will be able to understand what we originally meant when we wrote it.

Write it now, fix it later. We cannot begin editing our work until we first have a manuscript to edit. It can wait. Grammar, spelling, and punctuation can be corrected during our first rewrite. Yes, our first rewrite. We will spend much more time rewriting than writing.

EDITORS
I only mention this as a side note. Alpha readers, beta readers, and editors can be very helpful even in writing your second draft. It isn't written correctly if they don't understand what we wrote. Professionals and friends can help us find story gaps and technical gaffs.

VERBAL FEEDBACK

Have a friend read the work aloud. Make it a good friend, trust me; casual friends will give up quickly and try to convince us it's time to grab pizza and a beer. Hearing our story aloud brings rhythm and flow into the clear light of day. It'll also shine a bright light on glaring mistakes.

We all need to find someone we trust to let us know how well—or not—we are progressing. Writers don't write in a vacuum, unless they live in a vacuum. Read it aloud. It sounds strange, but it is very effective. We hear clearly what our eyes will not see on the written page.

Read it to someone. If someone says it doesn't sound right, they're probably correct, but if they tell us how to fix it, they are probably wrong. We write it our way, but listen to the criticism. By the way, if a person hates being criticized, they should seek another hobby. Writing isn't done without criticism.

Have someone read it aloud to us. It isn't funny if it doesn't make us laugh. It isn't tragic if it doesn't make us cry. We can even get a computer program to read it back to us, but we may miss the constructive criticism that way, not to mention voice inflection and emotion.

Reading aloud requires two copies of the story, one for the reader and one for the writer to annotate corrections or changes.

Reading aloud eliminates the tendency to skim the work as we read through where we have been. We have seen this story in our heads. We have a complete visual overview that may not have translated clearly to the written page. We may have reached a point where we read something that isn't there or we miss something we thought was there.

Readers
Search diligently for good readers. Just because someone has a college degree in French literature doesn't mean they enjoy a good horse opera. You should strive to find a reader for this task that understands what you want to say. This may be difficult. It means searching for a reader who reads the same genre you write. Take the time to give them a complete overview of the story. This isn't the time to hold back that surprise ending.

Strive to receive feedback from two types of readers:

- Alpha Readers – Our primary story content feedback readers. They can tell us where those main gaps lie and why this doesn't work because the hero's line of sight was blocked by the big multi-story building. These readers need to see our story before we fix grammar and punctuation because their feedback may cause us to dump paragraphs, shuffle pages, and rewrite entire chapters of our story. They often see our stories in small sections before we've even completed the manuscript.
- Beta Readers – Our secondary readers who focus on small story and plot gaps, contradictions, and wasted words. We want them to suggest what should be deleted and anything they would like to know more about.

Good alpha and beta readers are hard to find. Many publishers and agents keep such people on their staffs, but beginning authors may have limited access to them. We may have to search through crowds of readers to find the good ones. Cherish them when you do find them. Treat them well; buy them dinner every now and then. Thank them often; invite them to your holiday party. You get the picture.

There are professional alpha and beta readers. They can be very expensive and some are only there to help themselves into your money vault. Be wary. We should get references from writers we know about readers we don't.

Mom is a terrible critic, unless you have one of *those* mothers. My mother would tell me what I wrote was wonderful even if all I did was copy pages from the phonebook. That may stroke my ego, but it will not improve my writing. Generally, Aunt Dorothy will not be much better. Seek out the harsh critics. It is painful, but we will be better storytellers for the critique. Seek out the person who will tell us we have a booger hanging from our nose, it's embarrassing to hear, but they're telling us the truth to help us improve.

STORY GAPS
Story gaps are common among new writers. We can see the story in our imagination, but we struggle to find the correct words to describe adequately what we are seeing in a smooth, orderly manner. We may prefer writing in a vacuum, but our story will be better if we allow others to help us breathe life into it. Our alpha and beta readers are story gap investigators.

TECHNICAL GAFFS
A technical gaff would be where a friend or a not-so-friendly editor says, "Sorry, but that car never came with a standard, stick shift transmission." Double-check any and all technical descriptions. Keep records of your sources for future reference.

VOCABULARY

Keep a glossary of terms for our work if it involves *any* specialized vocabulary:

- Military terms
- Sports jargon
- Made up language
- Ethnic slang
- Historical period word use

A good writer uses a thesaurus to increase their vocabulary. Don't get bogged down searching for that perfect word on the first draft. We use the words we know. Correct during editing. We don't want to overuse terms or phrases, mix it up but retain the same flow or voice.

To read a writer is for me not merely to get an idea of what he says, but to go off with him and travel in his company. (Andre Gide)

SHOW, DON'T TELL

Write in the active tense, not the passive tense. For example: "Bob punched the obnoxious drunk", not "the obnoxious drunk was punched by Bob". Write to show activity, not pacifity.

We should always have something going on, even when we are describing things or our character is thinking.

SENTENCES

Our style is unique to us and it should be. We cannot separate our content from our style. It's what makes our books original and imaginative. Our sentence structure defines our style. Yet we should control our sentences, as it's often not what we say, but how we say it that matters to our reader. Our sentences give purpose to our writing. They add emotional dimensions to fulfill our reader's needs.

Sentence length is not a very useful index to style, but varying sentence length will add rhythm to our writing.

There are two varieties of sentences:
- Cumulative sentences build by adding subordinate clauses onto the base clause or even subordinate clauses onto other subordinate clauses. These often use free flowing prepositions or free modifiers. They can add texture, detail and motion to our sentence structure and syntax.
- Suspensive sentences leave information out. They are designed to entice our readers to keep reading.

RHYTHM

Even though we aren't writing poetry, prose does have a rhythm. Readers unconsciously hear this pattern in their favorite books. We have all heard the comment, "it was an easy read". This happens when the writer and the reader find common rhythmic ground.

Rhythm isn't as complete a mystery as many writers would have us believe. Rhythm is part of our voice, our style, and our literary persona. It's what makes reading Nathanial Hawthorne different than reading Ernest Hemingway.

Rhythm is found in our overall storyline. It's the variable pattern of getting our protagonist into and out of trouble. Our story progresses as a series of troubles and fixes: trouble, trouble, fix, trouble, trouble, fix, trouble, fix, trouble, fix, trouble, fix, fix, fix. Hear the rhythm?

Pace

Each writer determines the pace to their manuscript. The three elements of pace are commonly called scene, sequel, and the breath in between.

1. Scene – this is what happened in the action. This is when we throw trouble at our characters.
2. Sequel – this is the aftermath of what happened. This is when we help our characters get out of trouble.
3. Breath in between – The pause between action where we allow our readers to foolishly take a breath while we set them up for the next bit of action that will take their breath away. Note: we cannot take someone's breath away if they aren't breathing to begin with.

Word Flow
Rhythm is found within a paragraph as the words flow toward or away from the main subject of the paragraph. Does our paragraph hammer the first sentence and then relax in the remaining sentences, then hammer again at the beginning of the next paragraph only to relax again? This gives us a DAH-da-da-da; DAH-da-da-da; DAH-da-da-da rhythm. We may hit our imaginative stride when our rhythm is da-DAH-da-da.

Sentence Structure
Rhythm can be found most easily in a sentence structure. The more we write, the broader our experience, the more complete, more in depth and more complex sentences we will employ. Unfortunately, many writers believe the shorter a sentence is, the better it is. This may lead to using only a heartbeat rhythm: subject verb; subject verb; subject verb; da-DAH; da-DAH; da-DAH. This is a rock and roll rhythm. It is found in many science fiction and western novels. I'm not knocking it, I love this rhythm, it's a good rhythm, however it's simple and limiting in its affect on the reader.

Sentence Complexity
Complex sentences give us room to grow as writers. We begin our story with our base clause. It's our standard subject and verb structure. The modifying or subordinate clauses gives life, depth and rhythm to our base clause. This is a sentence from my novel *The Friendship Stones,* "White asters bloomed in a sprinkling across the meadow, landlocked constellations twinkling in the sunlight, dancing in the breeze to the music of the brook neatly dividing the meadow into equal halves."

The base clause is "White asters bloomed in a sprinkling across the meadow". For our rhythmic purposes we will

141

call our base clause *one*. This clause is a good start and is descriptive of the meadow. I wanted to give the reader more. As writers, we always want to give our readers more.

The first modifying or subordinate clause is "landlocked constellations twinkling in the sunlight". This clause modifies our base clause so we call it *two*.

The next modifying clause is "dancing in the breeze". This is also *two* as it modifies our base clause, *one*.

The next modifying clause is "to the music of the brook". This subordinate clause actually modifies the clause "dancing in the breeze". Since this clause modifies a *two* clause, we label it *three*. Not because it is the third modifier, but because a *three* clause modifies a *two* clause.

The final modifying clause is "neatly dividing the meadow into equal halves". This clause modifies the third subordinate clause by giving us a greater description of the brook. We call it a *four* because it modifies a *three* clause.

The numerical rhythm to this sentence is *one-two-two-three-four*. The next sentence in the paragraph was also a compound sentence with the same sequence. So the whole paragraph reads *one-two-two-three-four* and *one-two-two-three-four*. That is sentence rhythm.

We determine our own rhythms. Take the *one-two-three*, and *one-two-three*, and *one-two-three* rhythm as an example. This is a nice waltz rhythm.

What's Wrong

As writers, we will often stop and say, "I don't know what, but something is missing." A likely cause to our distress is that our rhythm is off. We may have written a *one-two-three-three-three-two-three-three-two-three-three-three* sentence. Simple analysis shows we are missing a *three* modifier in the second *two* subordinate clause. That missing *three* clause disturbs the rhythm of our story. The correct rhythm should be *one-two-three-three-three-two-three-three-three-two-three-three-three*.

5.2 WRITE FAST; REWRITE SLOW

I include this for completeness, please don't read this until you have completed the first draft of your first novel.

Really.

Quit reading now and go write.

EDITING
Write fast. Rewrite slowly. Once we have completed our first draft we should put it in the *cooler*. Write something else, read something, go do something else. Let it sit. Just like that gelatin dessert, allow the story set and cool a bit before attempting the first rewrite. This may be our first rewrite or the first of twenty-one editing reviews, but we need to let the story settle in our thoughts first.

Next step, read it as a reader, not as its writer.

As we learn editing, proofreading, proper grammar, punctuation, and formatting, we will also learn how and when we can break the rules of language. There are approximately 240 figures of speech in the English language. Figures of speech are deliberate violations of the laws of speech for emphasis. Learning some of them beyond the simile and metaphor can help us mature as writers. It can also confound an editor who only knows two figures of speech. See the Appendix for additional information on figures of speech.

Sit down and put down everything that comes into your head and then you're a writer. But an author is one who can judge his own stuff's worth, without pity, and destroy most of it. (Sidonie-Gabrielle Colette)

144

PROOFREADING

If our sentence makes sense without the word, then eliminate the word. Blank words are words that really have no meaning. They are your literary null set. One example is *that*. This word gives purpose to a phrase. It's one of the most overused words in English.

That versus Which
Write to avoid both when possible. We should always do a "which hunt" during the editing process. Simply perform a word search and fix all instances located where which is used improperly. Which always gives the reader a choice; for example:
- Which do you want, this or that?
- Which do you select, life or death?
- Which is your favorite, vanilla or chocolate?

Adverbs
Delete adverbs if the meaning of the sentence is not affected. If an engineer can make the machine run without a specific part, then the part isn't necessary. Adverbs are describing words and any word ending in –ly. If the verb is strong enough, it doesn't need the help.

Adverbs and adjectives slow down the action. The word *very* should be removed from a writer's vocabulary.

Small Words
Small words can have big meanings. There are a number of small words that can have a major impact on the meaning of a sentence, many are misused by speakers, readers and writers alike. Here are a few types to pay close attention to with examples:

1. Temporal: after, as, before, now, since, then, until, when, while
2. Local: before, thence, where, whither
3. Logical:
   a. Contrasting: although, but, else, much more, nevertheless, otherwise, though, yet
   b. Comparison: according as, also, as, as…so, even as, likewise, so likewise
   c. Continuation: again, and, moreover
   d. Reason: because, for, if, since
   e. Result: so, so then, then, therefore, wherefore
   f. Purpose: so, so that, that, to the end
   g. Qualifying: although, except, unless
4. Series: finally, first, last, last of all
5. Emphatic: especially, hereby, indeed, not only, only, therein, these, this

Substitute damn every time you're inclined to write very; your editor will delete it and the writing will be just as it should be. (William Allen White, erroneously attributed to Mark Twain)

Syllables
Never use a four-syllable word when a two-syllable word will do. We're telling a story, not bragging about our vocabulary.

Rewrite Often

Don't try to fix everything in one rewrite, edit more than once. Separate edits may include:

- Edit glaring mistakes
- Edit poorly chosen words
- Edit words used repetitively
- Edit spelling—use the spellchecker but don't trust it
- Edit grammar
- Edit punctuation

One at a Time
Try doing a final edit one sentence at a time, from the back to the front. This will help overcome the tendency to get re-involved in the story.

Emphasis
Remove italics or bold highlights used for emphasis. Fiction isn't written correctly if the reader has to see what should be emphasized.

Share
We should offer to edit other writers' work in exchange for their editing services on our work. It helps us become better writers.

PUNCTUATION
Punctuation emphasizes what is said and done. It isn't written correctly if the writer has to prove their point with an exclamation point. Learn when to properly use a semicolon and when to use a comma.

Writing is like shadow boxing. And editing is when the shadows fight back. (Adam Copeland)

GRAMMAR

Proper grammar will come with time or with an elementary school education, whichever came first. A good writer can tell a good story and do it within the proper confines of the grammar rules. Learn the rules of the written language. Learn to spell and do not rely solely on a computer spellchecker. Learn to build a perfect sentence without the use of a reference sheet. A successful writer should study grammar, we want to succeed so we should know the basics of grammar rules.

FORMATTING

Formatting varies depending on the publishing media. Ask a publisher for their guidelines. Select another publisher if they do not have written guidelines. Even e-book publishers should have guidelines.

AGENTS

The Catch-22 of publishing is:

- You cannot get an agent unless you have been published
- You cannot get published unless you have an agent

This is not strictly true. However, it does take patience and diligence to find out what makes a good agent. It takes even more to find one who fits our criteria.

PUBLISHERS AND PUBLISHING

Publishing fiction has more rules than Grandma ever did at the dinner table. Ask a prospective agent or publisher for their submission guidelines. They all have them. Don't fight against these guidelines, that is a sure fire method to add another letter to the rejection collection. Follow their guidelines to the letter and double, triple, quadruple check that you have done so.

148

Good publishers are harder to find than a non-runny nose during cold season. When we do get a good publisher, do not ever leave them hanging. Go to Minot, North Dakota in January or Phoenix, Arizona in August if they need we to go there for a book signing, a conference, or a convention. They have invested in us as much as we are invested in them.

PARTING WORDS

Writers write.

Consider our rules:

- Rule number one—There are no rules to writing fiction. Therefore, ignore all rules about writing— even this one. We write what we want to write.

- Rule number two—We can't fix what ain't been writ. So, write the story down, and fix the grammar later.

- Rule number three—We don't have to write our novel from the first word to the last period. It doesn't matter what order we write; just write.

- Rule number four—The story takes as long to tell as it takes. Write the story.

Participate in your own success.

If there's a book you really want to read, but it hasn't been written yet, then you must write it. (Toni Morrison)

Good luck.

Keep writing.

Keep telling yourself "I am a writer."

A professional writer is an amateur who didn't quit. (unknown, erroneously attributed to Richard Bach)

APPENDIX: FIGURES OF SPEECH

I'm including this section, not as a editing or grammar lesson, but to help get that first novel written and written well. Figures of speech are designed for adding emphasis, color, and flair to our writing.

All language is governed by law, but in order to increase the power of a word, or the force of an expression, these laws are designedly departed from, and words and sentences are thrown into and used in, new forms, or figures. (E.W. Bullinger, *Figures of Speech Used in the Bible)*

There are approximately two hundred and forty different figures of speech in the English language. Some of these figures have up to forty varieties within the figure. This is not a book on grammar or figures of speech, so I'll cover only a few here that may add that exciting touch to our book. For example, instead of writing, "The plant was dry and needed water.", using a figure of speech, we may write, "The plant was thirsty and demanded a good watering". Which sentence gives the reader a better visual picture?

Simile
Declaration that one thing resembles another.

Example: "He is like a dog."

Metaphor
Declaration that one thing is or represents another.

Example: "He is a dog."

Implication (Hypocatastatis)

Declaration that implies the resemblance or representation.

Example: "Dog!"

Allegory
Continued metaphor or implication.

Example: "He is a dog, leaving fleas in my bed and peeing in the backyard."

He isn't a real dog with flees. This allegory continues the metaphor by adding implications of the man's poor sexual prowess and bad personal habits.

Idiomatic Expression (Idioma)
Peculiar usage of words or phrases.

Example: "He put up with her."

This doesn't mean he literally put her up somewhere and then climbed up with her, but the American expression is that he tolerated some minor habit or irritating manner of hers. Every culture and society has their own unique expressions that may be lost on people not included in the group. I have an acquaintance who was born in New Zealand and lives in Australia. Her book takes place in the South Pacific, however one of her main characters travelled to the United States and was invited by an American to a deer party. It took more than one email to determine that she meant a bachelor or a stag party.

We may want to add a glossary at the back of our book if we anticipate an audience from a different culture than our story's society or timeframe. I did this specifically for my Ozark Mountain Series.

Many Ands (Polysyndeton)
The repetition of the conjunction 'and'.

Example: "The Beatles consisted of John Lennon and Paul McCartney and George Harrison and Ringo Starr."

The repetition of the word 'and' without a climax is a signal to the reader that this is not merely a listing of band members, but a signal to the reader to stop at each listing to consider and weigh each as having unique merit and not simply individual members of a group.

Like Sentence Beginnings (Anaphora)
The repetition of the same word at the beginning of successive sentences, thus adding emphasis to statements and arguments by calling special attention to them.

Example: "The witness saw the killing. The witness saw the killer. The witness picked him out of a police lineup. The witness identified him as her nephew. The witness is a deacon in her church. The witness is known for her truthfulness."

This repetition of the word witness is designed to add weight to her character and honesty, rather than just be a summary or listing of what she saw.

Climax (Gradation)
A repetition in successive sentences with the sense of going up or climbing up a ladder. A figure of words is a climax in grammar. A figure of the sense is a climax in rhetoric.

Example: "Add to your chore of feeding the horses, mucking out their stalls: to mucking out their stalls, cleaning the tack room: to cleaning the tack room, restacking the hay bales: to restacking the hay bales, brushing the horses: to brushing the horses, riding them for their exercise."

The repetition is a building of activities.

Unequal Yoked (Zeugma)
One verb is yoked to two unequal subjects.

Example: "He was of the Native American tribe that dwelt in tents and horses."

This is not grammatically wrong if it is done deliberately. Obviously, no one actually dwells in horses. Grammatically this would be written dwelt in tents and possessed horses, but written with the figure of speech gives emphasis to the subject's nomadic lifestyle of tents and horses.

Word Folding (Ploce)
Repetition of the same word in the same sentence with different meanings.

Example: "My wife is a wife indeed."

The first use of the word wife gives us her place in our relationship. The second use of the word wife is used to emphasis all of the things a wife should be.

Exaggeration (Hyperbole)
When more is said than is literally meant.

Example: "He left his parents behind and gave his service to the Army."

This is not to imply that he no longer loved or cared about his parents or that he forsook them.

Word Picture (Hypotyposis)
Describes an action, event, person, condition, passion, image, or thought in a lively and forcible manner.

Example: "Her desire to marry was a team of draft horses pulling her along."

A desire has no physical form or shape, yet with this figure of speech, we can give it one and give our reader a mental picture.

Description of Character (Characterismos)
Description of manners.

Example: "He was a cold boss."

This adds emphasis to his aloofness, not his temperature.

Personification
Adding human characteristics to aliens, animals, or elements of nature.

Example: "The wind wrapped its powerful arms around the barn and squeezed, giving the roof its freedom."

The wind doesn't have arms and roofs are inanimate objects that do not require freedom.

Wise Folly (Oxymoron)
A wise saying that seems foolish.

Example: "The light in his heart was as dark as a moonless night."

Light cannot be dark. We can find this figure of speech in contradictory words or phrases such as cruel kindness, hasten slowly, or lost foundling.

Irony (Eironeia)
An expression of thought in a form that conveys its opposite.

Example: "Settle down, people. This court of vengeance is now in session."

Substituting vengeance for justice adds irony to the official proceedings. Sarcasm is a form of irony when it is used as a taunt or in ridicule.

Reference: *Figures of Speech Used in the Bible*, E.W. Bullinger, Published by Baker Book House, Grand Rapids, Michigan, ISBN 0-8010-0559-0

About the Author:
www.alanblackauthor.com

Alan Black has been writing novels since 1997 when he started *Eye on The Prize*. His writing tastes are as eclectic as his reading preferences. Alan admits that he loves writing much more than editing and the whole publishing process.

Alan was born in central Kansas and grew up in Gladstone, Missouri. He graduating from Oak Park Senior High School and eventually earning a liberal arts degree from Longview Community college. He spent most of his adult life in the Kansas City area. The exception came at the orders from the U.S. Air Force when he was stationed in Texas, California, Maryland, and Japan. He and his wife were married in the late 70s and moved back to Independence, Missouri, but now live in sunny Arizona.

His desire to write started in the second grade. He was given an assignment to write a short story about Greek mythology. His teacher took the time to call his parents and express her appreciation of the story. Although neither of his patents remembered the incident, it had an impact on him, eventually leading him to write *Eye On The Prize*, taking two years to complete. He has gotten faster since then completing a recent manuscript in three weeks.

Alan Black is a #1 bestselling author for *Metal Boxes*, a young adult, science fiction, military, action adventure. He has published ten novels to date. He is an indie multi-genre writer who has never met a good story he didn't want to tell.

Alan Black's vision statement: "I want my readers amazed they missed sleep because they could not put down one of my books. I want my readers amazed I made them laugh on one page and cry on the next. I want to give my readers a pleasurable respite from the cares of the world for a few hours. I want to offer stories I would want to read."

Praise for Alan Black's books

Titanium Texicans
Alan Black's work will suck you in!

I am not good at reviews, but this is the third work of Mr. Black's that I have read in three weeks because his writing captures my imagination. I like good space operas because they last longer, but Black's stand alone works are great because they leave me satisfied at the end and not disappointed that there isn't more to come.

Titanium Texicans is a page-turner full of authentic dialogue with concepts greater than the satisfying amount of sci-fi technology woven into a well-written coming of age story. Take the time to read it. I certainly wasn't sorry that [I] did.

Amazon review by MC on June 13, 2015

Metal Boxes
Good Sci-fi Adventure Fun All Around

If you like good engaging reading with a fun story and characters you can like, this is it. Overall everything works together to create an absolutely fun sci-fi read.

The hard science fiction aspect in space is interesting as it brings some new elements to FTL travel in a survival mode – think life raft in the middle of the ocean with a tiny battery operated motor.

The other world science fiction is equally fun as are the new species and their peculiarities.

The story is multi-tiered just enough to keep the pace interesting and dramatic. The hero is unlikely in so many ways it would be implausible except that he has both life long history of superior knowledge and genetics on his side that makes it all work quite well. For this I give the author excellent marks because it adds an element of humanity to a genre that too often has super heroes who are just a bit too super.

The action and pace of the story are just about perfect. Not once did I find my attention faltering – and I am rather difficult to please on this issue. For that alone Metal Boxes is worth the time and money.

However, good pacing is not the only stellar issue. All of the writing is tight and clean. In a time of many new self-published authors who don't take their trade quite seriously enough, Mr. Blacks books are a joy to read. This is the third book of his I have read. I have been happy with each one and will continue with his others.

Amazon review by Sandy on September 28, 2014

The Friendship Stones

This is a truly wonderful story for the whole family!

What a great story! *The Friendship Stones* is an uplifting story of twelve year old LillieBeth and her life in the Ozarks. The setting takes place in the early part of the twentieth century between World War 1 & 2. This was a very challenging time to the economy of the U.S.A. and the world. Epidemics of illness plus war had impacted many. The lives and hearts of a vast portion of societies were suffering and people were struggling to survive.

The two authors- Alan Black & Bernice Knight - effectively illustrated the prevailing challenges of that time well. Written in the first person, LillieBeth and her family easily captivated the heart of the reader. Equally effective and realistic were the other supporting characters. One scene smoothly and steadily flowed into another, keeping the reader's undivided attention.

It is ideal for any Christian or non-Christian audience. I can hardly wait to read the next book of the series. *The Friendship Stones* gives one a feeling of *The Little House on the Prairie* moments. Main topics were coming of age, family unity, Ozark community, trying times.

This is definitely a Five Stars rated book.

Amazon review by LAWonder on September 27, 2014

The Granite Heart
Heartwarming Historical Fiction

Alan Black takes us back to the 1920's, to the Ozark Mountains, and back into the world of twelve year old LillieBeth Hazkit, who tries to live by the teachings of God, but finds life can sometimes be confusing, brutal and too unforgiving to always accept that God has a plan for all contingencies. Her strange hermit-like friend has been killed, her teacher has lost her job through no fault of her own and the impoverished mountain town becomes a colder and less friendly place for someone with a heart as big as LillieBeth's. The archaic and small-minded double standards set her teeth on edge and she is determined to stand strong and be heard, no matter what. The men who murdered her friend and raped her teacher have been captured, but enroute to the county seat they escape and kill one man while injuring her father. To LillieBeth, justice must be done, plain and simple and she and her former teacher, Susanne Harbowe set out on an impossible mission to hunt down and capture these monsters.

Told from Susanne's point of view, LillieBeth's story takes on a new depth as she makes her mark on the hearts and minds of those who know her. Alan Black has created a warm and inviting tale that places the reader back in time, to a place so remote, it's almost as if the rest of the world does not exist. Simple joys, complicated pain and a loss of childhood innocence shake LillieBeth's world and harden her heart, while forcing her into the world of adults.

Alan Black creates a world filled with history, rich in detail and well-developed characters that worm their way into your heart and mind. That I could feel LillieBeth's feelings and see what she saw is the mark of an amazing author who deserves to be read.

Amazon review by Dii (TOP 500 REVIEWER) on August 22, 2014

The Heaviest Rock

Strength of character and a easy manner to it that catches and keeps you.

This series is one of the most enjoyable ones I have read. It has heart, action, humor, strength of character and a easy manner to it that catches you and keeps you right there through till the end. Can't wait for the next one ' wiggles on' for those of you who don't know what this means I guess you will just have to get the book and find out for yourself, big hint it is so worth it !!!

Amazon review by Tammie on March 2, 2015

Empty Space

Really cool sci-fi read!!

York Sixteen grew up in a system that didn't treat orphans well. They were abused in the worst of ways by anyone and everyone. They could never climb the social ladder no matter how hard they tried. They were nobodies and always would be. York is a survivor though. He does what he has to, but even his best isnt good enough when he loses his top ranking in the military school on the day he graduates. As a result of being at the top and an orphan, he was set up and ultimately stripped of his rank. Eventually he's assigned to a remote area far away in space. A true touch-me-not, being alone doesn't bother York that much. However he does need some human contact and finally begins a tentative friendship with a few people who live on the planet he's closest to. Plagued by those kidnapping people for the slave trade, York finally finds his purpose in helping them gain their freedom from these slavers.

My thoughts on York—he's a serial killer with justification; kind of a vigilante. He rids society of the trash it won't take care of, which is mainly anyone helping make the rich and powerful more rich and powerful. No one on the planet Liberty exactly adheres to the law. They do what they have to survive. They're York's kind of people. As a consequence of being stationed where he was, he finds things he had been missing his whole life: friendship, acceptance, a love interest, and a purpose. This guy has a serious dark side to him, but it all stems from his childhood,

I'm pretty sure. Alan Black created a complicated character with York Sixteen. He's sort of a dark knight mixed in with Star Wars. I would say that York is very much like the conflicted Anakin on Star Wars before he becomes Darth Vader.

A very cool sci-fi read no doubt! 5 out of 5 stars!!

Chasing Harpo

Soldiers from Rwanda were in the area. Police knew they were gang related. No one could ever imagine the chain of events that would take place over the next few days. Carl knew nothing about the gang. He was trying to get up nerve to ask Terri out. Then it happened. Now the police are chasing Carl and his friend Harpo with orders to shoot on sight. Can Carl keep Harpo safe? With a little help he just might be able to make this right.

A fun read that, for me, was like checkin' up on relatives from the south! *smile* Well written and characters you'll love, this book will bring a smile to your face. Mr. Black does a wonderful job of making this book come alive. I do recommend it. I found no issues.

I gave this one 5 cheers out of 5 because I smiled and giggled through much of the book.

A Cold Winter

Great job, Mr. Black.
Mr. Black writes with such realism. He's definitely a true storyteller. Mr. Black has invited the reader to take a journey into the world of a brave woman named Libby.

The stage is set for one lone woman's difficulties in facing a hard cold winter from the beginning of page one. The writing captivated me from the start. Mr. Black's attention to detail puts the reader right next to his character.

Great job, Mr. Black. Looking forward to reading more of your work.

Chewing Rocks

A strong female character you can't help but love

Chastity Snowden Whyte had gotten into too much trouble trying to defend her name and so started going by Sno. What a great name. Sno! Isn't that a weather condition, people ask when first introduced to her, many of whom have never seen snow, being born somewhere off planet, planet Earth, that is? Sno, herself, had only heard stories of snow, having been born on a planetoid somewhere between Mars and Jupiter. In the opening chapter, Alan Black paints an out-of-this-world picture of young Sno busy outside her spacecraft in her EVA suit, by herself, mining asteroids for rock and hopefully, a rare metal or two. When she returns to her home base in Arizona City on a small planetoid called, Ceres, she gets in a barroom scrap with 4 fellow miners from a competing operation. Without harming so much as a fingernail, she puts them in their place and then shortly after blasts off into the asteroid belt again to work a claim. It's what happens when they chase after her that makes Chewing Rocks so much fun to read. Great action, wonderful word visuals of the planetoid city, the spaceships and the mining operations along with a multitude of colorful characters made Chewing Rocks hard to walk away from. When I got to the arbitration scenes with Therese Cleasemount, I just simply couldn't put my iPad down; actually found myself chuckling now and then. I think maybe our justice system could learn a little bit from Miss Cleasemount.

Chewing Rocks was simply a joy to read. I look forward to reading more about Chasity Snowden (Sno) Whyte.

Steel Walls and Dirt Drops
Another masterpiece as far as I am concerned. What a masterful use of characters! Kept me on the edge of my chair, I could not wait to see what was going to happen next. It is a great mix of people problems, engineering, and science fiction. I would love to see the movie. Great work, Alan!

Amazon review by Larry Wright on March 20, 2015

CPSIA information can be obtained
at www.ICGtesting.com
Printed in the USA
FSHW021321070120
65832FS

9 781511 522939